Get a Grip

Get a Grip

Your Two-Week Mental Makeover

Dr. Belisa Vranich

WILEY

John Wiley & Sons, Inc.

Published by John Wiley & Sons, Inc., Hoboken, New Jersey
Published simultaneously in Canada

The information contained in this book is not intended to serve as a replacement for professional medical advice. Any use of the information in this book is at the reader's discretion. The author and the publisher specifically disclaim any and all liability arising directly or indirectly from the use or application of any information contained in this book. A health care professional should be consulted regarding your specific situation.

For general information about our other products and services, please contact our Customer Care Department within the United States at (800) 762-2974, outside the United States at (317) 572-3993, or fax (317) 572-4002.

Wiley also publishes its books in a variety of electronic formats. Some content that appears in print may not be available in electronic books. For more information about Wiley products, visit our Web site at www.wiley.com.

Library of Congress Cataloging-in-Publication Data:

Lozano-Vranich, Belisa, date.
  Get a grip : your two-week mental makeover / Belisa Vranich.
    p. cm.
  Includes index.
    ISBN 978-0-470-38319-3 (hardback)
  1. Self-actualization (Psychology) I. Title.
  BF637.S4L7 2010
  158.1—dc22

                                                        2009028770

Printed in the United States of America
10 9 8 7 6 5 4 3 2 1

This erraticism is a normal part of getting unstuck, pulling free from the muck that has blocked us. It is important to remember that at first flush, going *sane* feels just like going crazy.

—Julia Cameron, *The Artist's Way*

CONTENTS

vii

PREFACE

As a therapist, the one thing I do in therapy that is really important is to encourage patients to listen—to themselves. As an adult, you've taught yourself that you are not supposed to let your thoughts go off in that "forbidden" direction, or you may believe that you've gotten over that hurtful incident long ago. But let me tell you that in the therapy room, the rule is that there are no rules. Every worry you have, every hope you've quashed, every vindictive or ridiculous fantasy you've entertained has a place. In this book you will learn that once you voice those thoughts—or write them down—you will have the *choice* of what to do with them. You might figuratively take an idea out from that box under the bed and put it on the mantle. You might compare it to information you have now, years later, and then decide you can throw it out. You might find that it's not a tantalizing notion anymore, or you might discover that it's the opposite—that it's a dream you have to live out before you die.

Ideally the perfect combination is a live therapy session reinforced by your own work day to day. That "work" might be not letting others get you down, or being honest and forgiving regardless of the reactions of others. That work may be finding something to appreciate every day or to practice random acts of kindness, confidently following Mother Teresa's words "Do it anyway," even if those acts haven't made their way back around to you as you've been promised. Maybe it is just not beating yourself up for your mistakes, or staying in the present "just for today," and not ruminating about the past or worrying about the future. You don't have to be in therapy, however, to want to better yourself or to find situations therapeutic.

Continually striving to be a better human being is exhausting. You'll have moments when you think that people who are cantankerous, rigid, or self-involved seem to have it easy. They don't strive, so they don't fail. They are so removed or engrossed in themselves that they don't register discomfort or pain around them. However, when you start cleaning up *your* world, start trying to be a better person, to be more appreciative, more kind, and more in tune, that is when you may notice that the sweet moments are even more vivid than before. You'll find yourself humming along with the U2 song "It's a Beautiful Day" because you know that worry will cloud your vision from seeing that it is in fact a beautiful day, and if you don't take time to notice it, you'll blink and you are ten years older, then blink again and you are twenty, and so on.

In these pages you will find a tough psychological work-out, with guidelines on how to solve the emotional problems that you've been carrying around, that have been weighing you down, and that nag you when you go to bed. These problems may have legitimate-sounding labels like "lack of closure," "bereavement," or "abandonment issues," but they are missing the instructions on how to work your way through them. If you do the work in this book whole-heartedly, it will start you moving in the right direction, get you out of that rut, and resolve that quandary. This book will give you the means to answer the existential questions you are grappling with (What can I do to be happier? How do I live in a more balanced way? Where should I be going to from here?) or the specific ones that are gnawing away at you every day (Am I meant to be with my partner? Why can't I lose weight? Should I stay at this job?). Allowing yourself to take the time to read this book and to follow its instructions unconditionally will be life changing: you'll have a better perspective, recognize options you didn't know existed, or maybe just wake up in the morning feeling more optimistic about the day ahead of you.

There are things that I left out of this book. When I began to write it, I wanted to be able to mention everything I ever found useful so that you could have it, too. I wanted, as I do with my patients, to be able to tailor the work so it would fit your personality. I wanted to be able tell you that in addition to the classic therapy work, given your personality, to read *Passionista* to help your relationship and anything by Thich Nhat Hanh, see the documentary *My Mother's Garden* to better understand your mom's "collecting," take that tango class, and before your next session visit your father's grave. No excuses! Or maybe, to make you see something you didn't understand yet or to tell you to ask your siblings for their version of what happened that fateful summer, call you-know-who and tell him or her what you really think of that person, and ditch your sadistic diet for the next week until this "bump" is over. I wanted to tailor it for each and every reader, and I think that I found a way to do that by creating exercises that make you adapt the self-therapy for your unique self.

As is the case with most patients at the beginning of therapy, you are itching to ask me, "Am I normal?" And I have to tell you, I already know that you are not. You wanted me to say that, yes, within a range of normal behavior, of normal adults, you fall sometimes to the left or sometimes to the right, but you are in that spectrum. "I knew it," you are thinking. "I knew I was weird," you say. The fact is, you are not reading this because you want to be normal; you are reading this because you want to be *better*. Already in that regard you are above average. It's human nature to settle, to procrastinate, to cram feelings and experiences into the Pandora's boxes in our memories, and push them to the back of the drawer under the socks. You hear yourself think, "But what if I . . .," and you shush that voice. You affirm you are content, or at least doing just fine, over and over, hoping you'll believe it. But you know that deep down you want more.

So stop complaining about the world around you, grab this book, and start working on yourself to be a little microcosm of the world the way you wish it was. What you now have in your hands is the next best thing to having your own personal therapist. Whatever changes you desire—better relationships, reconciliation with the past, insight into a persistent existential question, or a more joyful life—you can make them. You will now learn how to expand that circle, and expand it again and again. With my help and your commitment, you will put a plan into action, make the necessary changes, make sure the ripples of your actions don't hurt anyone, and learn to find strength to be a better person by looking inside of yourself, where your strength really lies.

Ultimately, the answers all come from within; you just need the right questions. Turn the page, and let's start.

INTRODUCTION

Lost Your Grip?

My style of therapy has always been holistic and psychodynamic—a "think-outside-the-office" approach in which homework and taking responsibility are critical. When the book *Eat, Pray, Love* by Elizabeth Gilbert gained great popularity, I found that many patients—both men and women—wanted to know how they could "find themselves," as the protagonist did.

Finally, what pushed me to start writing *Get a Grip* was running into a neighbor, Maria Dahvana Headley, who wrote a book called *The Year of Yes* about how she decided to say yes to every man who asked her out on a date. It forced her to reevaluate her "requirements" and start thinking differently. She said that readers were exasperated to find that she didn't have any advice specifically for them. "This was just my story; they need to find their own," she said.

I figured I'd write a workbook to help people write their own story. I wanted to give people who are curious about psychology but don't currently have the time or means to go into therapy some therapeutic work they could do on their own. Although a book cannot reproduce an actual relationship with a therapist, it can ask important questions that stimulate critical answers and lead to extremely important realizations and themes.

You are about to become your own therapist. You probably have at least one stress-related pain, one big regret, or one recurring emotional topic you wish you could resolve. Face it: we all have things about ourselves that we'd like to change, relationships we'd like to be smoother, a past we'd like to be more at peace with, or an existential question that we'd like to be closer to answering. Contrary to what you might believe, not everyone comes to therapy with career-changing questions or tons of baggage from a childhood trauma. Sometimes people just want to feel happier or more balanced. Sometimes they just want to be less irritable, have clarity about the next few years of their lives, or simply be able to see the glass as half full, not half empty. At other times people just want to feel better in some general way.

The problem is that the unconscious is dark. The path taken to get to the here and now was tumultuous. Everyone wants to be able to lose weight effortlessly, quit smoking easily, or fall asleep quickly, but it doesn't always happen. In a culture where people are obsessed by measurable outcomes, the deeper quest to nurture their "inner child," to "find themselves," or to integrate their mind, body, and soul has been replaced by a frantic push for instant results. As seductive as a quick fix might be, the problem is that in most cases it just doesn't work.

Traditional therapy can provide a genuine opportunity for profound and lasting change, but it may not be right for you at this time. Maybe you are surrounded by friends who are comfortable comparing notes from their therapists over lunch. Perhaps you absolutely pooh-pooh therapy and think that venting to a friend or going to church does you just as much good. Maybe you'd like to go to a professional but can't stomach shelling out that kind of money to have someone sit across from you for forty-five minutes and simply listen—and then call it a therapeutic hour. Perhaps things just haven't gotten bad enough, and you're hoping that your problems will somehow figure themselves out or disappear if you ignore them long enough. Maybe it's a totally different situation: you *are* in therapy, but you feel as though you've reached a plateau and want to take it further somehow, or your therapist is on vacation or maternity leave.

So what are you going to do? The quick fixes haven't worked; the prospect of lengthy, expensive therapy is unappealing; and you want to take the opportunity to do some work on yourself, by yourself. This book offers you a way. It provides you with a unique approach that is profound and potentially life-changing. It takes you through the steps of what would happen in therapy sessions with a psychologist.

You don't have to wait for an ultimatum from your spouse, for panic attacks, for you to be the "right" age, for insurance that will cover the cost, or for the shrink with the right approach for you. There is no more stalling, waiting, groaning, and making excuses. Start your own therapy now. This book asks questions without judgment of any kind and without the constraints of the date and time of a therapy session. It is an innovative self-therapy approach.

People often come to therapy because they feel restless, are in limbo, or are wondering, "Is this as good as it gets?" In your case, maybe it's just that you see other people having fun and you're asking yourself why you're not one of them. Maybe things just don't seem right: you cry at the drop of a hat, you can't let things go, you have regrets, or you can't figure out how to stop the merry-go-round and get off. Does this sound familiar? Read on.

I'll take you through the steps of what would happen in therapy sessions. This self-therapy, like traditional therapy, has the goal of achieving insight and understanding. Although some concepts, like transference (the patient's emotional reaction to the therapist) and countertransference (the therapist's emotional reaction to the patient) are logistically impossible to explore in this book, other concepts can be maximized in a way never attempted before.

Get a Grip works because it asks the questions that will force you to reassess and shift. The main body of the text is meant to shake or rev up your emotions. The assignments will show you how to achieve change. Along the way you'll have moments of clarity, and memories will bubble up. Eventually you'll reach conclusions that, strangely enough, will feel familiar, as though you knew they were there all along—they were just buried deep inside you, out of reach.

My approach is psychodynamic, which means that behavior and mental states are explained in terms of mental and emotional forces or processes, including early childhood influences and unconscious motivation. It draws from several modes of therapy that focus on eradicating negative thinking patterns, irrational thoughts, and distressing memories of early relationships with one's family, in addition to some insights from Eastern and Western philosophies. Step by step, the chapters will empower you so that you can discover the solutions yourself.

The answers to your questions are wrapped up in the story of your childhood, buried in your dreams, secreted in the way you think and in how you perceive yourself. I will give you the tools to challenge your old definitions of yourself, disentangle fixed ideas, chip away at the emotional walls you've erected, and make space in your head for clearer and more optimistic thoughts so that you can make smarter decisions about your future.

I will teach you to do what a therapist does: ask questions, retrieve memories, and confront what you believe to be true so that the inertia you are experiencing starts to give way. Rather than continuing to look outside yourself for clues about what you should do, you'll learn that achieving a peaceful balance comes after you recognize the answers you hold within. When you go to therapy, a therapist listens, "mirrors," interprets, and asks questions that lead you to an "Aha!" moment, when all the dots connect. If you are willing to do the work, follow the steps that challenge you, and do the prescribed emotional problem solving in a focused way, this book will bring you to an "Aha!" moment, too—or rather, *you* will bring yourself to it.

The most common complaint that patients voice in therapy is that they find it difficult to change their behavior. Understanding in and of itself can often bring an abrupt halt to the therapeutic process. A person feels relief at the brief control that he or she experiences, and his or her motivation therefore wanes. In addition, a therapist has to respect the pace at which patients make self-discoveries. This means choosing when to challenge their defenses yet being nonjudgmental at all times. My method doesn't have those limitations; it can be very direct in its instructions for change. These pages will "talk" to you—they might even yell a little, reprimand at times, console when necessary, and cheer when you are close to the end.

Get a Grip does not contain any magical therapy secrets, nor does it encourage you through tough love to pull yourself up by your own bootstraps. This is an intensive two-week therapy workbook that offers practical, cut-to-the-chase instructions that are not for the fainthearted. Each chapter proceeds in a way similar to that of a weekly therapy session. You'll have no need to be embarrassed, hesitant, or ashamed to answer the questions, because *you* are asking them. You will, at some point, I am sure, be surprised at your answers and the results—and relieved. First, however, you have to commit to starting. Have you done so?

DAY ONE

How Self-Analysis Works

Visualize yourself in a therapist's office, on your first day in therapy. Does your therapist look like Sigmund Freud? A TV character like Dr. Melfi or Frasier? Or a famous media personality like Dr. Drew, Dr. Phil, Dr. Laura, Dr. Ruth, Dr. Keith Ablow, or Dr. Sanjay Gupta? You might be excited, nervous, or skeptical. It may feel vaguely like an interview for a new job. Will the therapist like you? Where do you sit? How do you start? What are the rules? Forty-five minutes may seem infinitely long or be the shortest time you've ever experienced. Maybe you are feeling slightly guilty that this time is going to be devoted just to you—only you. You can ramble, babble, hum, or just sit and smile in silence at the person in front of you.

Nowhere else but in therapy does someone listen to you so intently. Your therapist remembers names, places, and events and offers you connections among them. A therapist hangs on to your every word. This method is at the heart of therapy: it is firmly based on the idea that words can reveal what is deep inside your unconscious. The answer to whatever you are struggling with is in the information your words impart.

What poses the challenge for a therapist is that a patient offers bits and pieces of a life that are not in a logical order, that have to be conflated and merged into a unified saga. Characters or details might be omitted; events seem to jump back and forth, from one year to the next. Sometimes what is *not* said can be a very important piece of the puzzle. A therapist will note your choice of words, the inflections, the repetitions. Depending on the approach the therapist is taking, he or she may mirror, interpret, or refute what you say. With this back-and-forth method, you'll arrive at a moment of truth.

The crucial step is right at the beginning. Just the fact that you decided to start the quest means that you will be able to find an answer, discover the truth, and make more informed choices than you ever have before. In a similar way, your picking up this book is that first step.

The question, then, is this: How can this book help you to achieve a breakthrough? The answer is, by the very methods used in therapy. As you advance day to day, the assignments will make the same queries and probe for the same answers that a therapist would. Words—your words, your remembering and writing down your thoughts—are the crux of this book.

You get as much out of traditional therapy as you put into it. The same is true with this book. If you skim the pages while you're watching TV and snacking, don't expect miracles. If you read carefully and jot down notes, seriously study your own thoughts as you would in a writing class, and question yourself with a view to doing a thorough examination of your thoughts, then you can expect to be both surprised and satisfied by what you discover, by finally knowing what actually makes you tick.

How, you might ask, can I be two people, both the therapist and the patient, the listener and the speaker? It's true that being an objective listener to your own story is difficult. You might not like what you're hearing, because in doing this work, you are going to have to learn to confront yourself, to pin yourself down when you are being belligerent, and to detect when you are hedging or lying.

The payoff is worth it. It is an incredibly satisfying moment when, in therapy, whether it's on the first day or in the first month, you realize something. It feels amazing to have one of those "Yes!" moments, when you jump up with your fist in the air. When you come across the answers that are important, you will feel it in your gut—undeniably.

The Rules

Every day you'll write in your journal for the same amount of time you would spend in a therapy session—forty-five minutes. The time of day is up to you. Are you more of a morning person? Is it easier to have uninterrupted "me time" in the evening, before going to bed? The key to picking your time is that for the next fourteen days, barring a fire in your building or your wife starting to have contractions, you have to keep your appointment. Momentum and the cumulative effect of doing this work every day are very important.

As you read this book, use the margins for writing notes whenever something catches your attention and really resonates with you; however, your journal is where you will expand and elaborate. Pick a very secure place to put your journal. Many a relationship has been ruined by a significant other reading something that his or her eyes weren't meant to see. If you are afforded the luxury of privacy, I suggest you keep your journal by your bedside at night.

Keep something to write on with you at all times in order to jot down notes during the day, then transfer them to your journal later or use them to start a new idea. Pick a space, a quiet spot in which to write, whether it's a room or a park. You should also write down your appointments with yourself. Yes, you do indeed make an appointment with yourself each day for the fourteen days. It isn't silly. Remember that you are following the same procedures as those used in clinical therapy, in which appointments, promptness, and commitment are key elements for success.

Here, in short, is the procedure you will follow:

1. This is a fourteen-day course. Every day counts. Commit to writing, even when you are tired, hung over, uninspired, or angry. It is exactly like going to the gym: you don't want to go, but you know you should; then you go, and you feel better.

2. This is a forty-five-minute session that is to be unin-terrupted, just like a therapy session. In therapy, you are paying for every minute, even if you cancel or are late, so use every minute carefully. Guard the time of your appointment—it might be the most productive and meaningful forty-five minutes of your day. It's sacred. During your writing time, your door should

be closed; do not peek out to see what's going on. Don't take phone calls, read text messages, or take coffee breaks. Do your business, and I mean *all* of your business, before you sit down for your session.

3. Write down *everything*, even if that means saying things that sound stupid, immature, egotistical, or rude. Let it all out. At times it may make no sense; at other times it may hurt or even shock you. You might repeat the same sentence over and over. It doesn't mean that you are unimaginative; it means that that particular sentence, that topic, or that issue is important.

4. Make this commitment your mantra: "I need to do this seriously for the next fourteen days so that I can feel better and figure things out. This is essential to my mental health, which is linked to my physical health. This is probably the most important thing I will do today, no matter how trivial it seems. I can take forty-five minutes out of my day for me. I need to do this."

5. Write down the ugly things. Use the strongest words that you know the topic deserves. People often don't write down their greatest fears because they think that giving them attention of any sort will make them happen or grow. This is not true. Don't be afraid to expand on the thought.

6. Don't let yourself talk yourself out of it. You may know yourself better than anyone, but you are also your biggest saboteur. Don't tell yourself that this is not working, that it's too late, or that it's an exercise in futility. Prevail even if you still haven't had an "Aha!" moment. It will come to you when it is right, and that might just be tomorrow.

ASSIGNMENT

Make the commitment to self-therapy just as you would with a therapist. Actually write it down. Reread the six points above, if you need to—do it as many times as necessary to reinforce your commitment. For today, just see which of the following most common therapy questions resonate with you. The forty-five minutes of writing will start tomorrow.

Common Therapy Questions

Following are the twenty most common topics that are brought to therapy (with variations of each). As you read them, circle the ones that make you nod and say, "Yes, that's me."

1. How can I find something I can be truly excited about? How can I be more motivated? I feel stuck in life. I feel a lack of passion in my life for anything. I'm not sure I like who I've become. I want to be happy.

2. What is my purpose in life? Is there some goal that I should be striving for that will bring me more satisfaction in my life? I feel as if everything I have worked for is meaningless—I want to make a difference in the world.

3. Why is it so hard to forgive?

4. I have such low self-esteem; how do I learn to love myself more? I want to be more confident.

5. How do I achieve more balance in my life? It seems that once I get over one crisis, another arises. I want less drama in my life.

6. Can I reparent myself? My biological family is nuts, and I want to make a new family of my own. Can my friends really be the family I choose?

7. How do I pick better romantic partners? I'm always trying to fix the people I date. Can I get my significant other to change what seems to be ingrained behavior?

8. I can't seem to commit. At what point in a relationship should I know that it's time to break it off? I feel trapped in my relationship. I can't figure out if I should stay or go. I feel increasingly detached from my partner.

9. How do I get over the latest breakup? How do I get closure?

10. Why do I often get upset or angry over the small stuff?

11. Why do I feel so guilty when I make mistakes? Why do I beat myself up so much?

12. Why do I work so hard to avoid conflict? Why do I find it so hard to stand up for myself? I want to be more assertive.

13. Why do I find it so difficult to accept my parents for who they are?

14. How can I continue to work at a job that I hate? I need the money, but I want to change jobs. I'm scared.

15. Why do I have so many regrets? Have I made bad decisions?

16. Why do I feel so mortal, that life is passing me by? I'm scared of aging.

17. Why do I feel so anxious? I worry so much.

18. Why do I feel like crying all the time?

19. Why can't I find the reason for my headaches, back-aches, or stomachaches?

20. Why do I compare myself to others so much? Why can't I accept myself as I am? How do others experi-ence me?

Whether you circle 19 of these 20, or just one, these perplexing, even tormenting, questions can be unraveled. You don't have to live with the uncertainty forever. Let's get moving.

DAY TWO

Venting: Let It All Hang Out

Venting is one of the most basic parts of therapy. Everyone vents. Usually a monologue about the day's injustices, venting serves a legitimate and healthy purpose: it chronicles the chaos. When you vent in therapy, you give free rein to your pent-up emotions. All of those choked-up feelings come gushing out, and you actually experience a physical response that lets you relax after a rant about the day's events.

You appreciate people who allow you to vent to them: your work buddy, your best friend, your roommate, a bartender. Just their nods of apparent agreement make venting so much more satisfying than grumbling to yourself. Responses from this type of audience vary from understanding sighs, expressions of exasperation

15

that match yours, noncommittal reflexive questions like "People are crazy, huh?" or sympathetic comments like "Wow, I feel for you." Chattier listeners might even want to participate, adding a similar story or their two cents about what you should do. (Admit it, however; their comments are more annoying than anything else. You just want to let off steam, uninterrupted.)

Venting on a daily basis is not only recommended, it's healthy. In effect, you are letting the air out of the soon-to-pop balloon that has been inflated by all of the emotional pressure inside you. (You've heard about people who are hesitant to talk because they've been bottling it up so long they are afraid they'll explode, haven't you?) Venting in therapy sounds similar, but the process is much more complex. As a psychologist, I listen intently to what patients say, but I also note how they react to their own verbal outpouring. The initial effect is the aforementioned physical relaxation that takes place. Airing your complaints is important because it allows you to unwind.

The patient is hardly passive in this process. As a person listens to himself talking about an issue, he notices how long he carries on about it and how exasperated or angry he sounds. From session to session, the patient may realize that he is stuck on a topic ("I sound exactly like last week, huh?" or "Hey, I sound like a broken record."). He may notice that he repeats the same theme, just changing the people involved ("Funny, I used the same words when I talked last month about So-and-So, didn't I?"). That's because he's hearing his own voice tell the story. Articulating an issue aloud is significantly different from just letting it run around and around on a hamster wheel inside your head.

Finally, stating your grievances often allows you to put them in perspective. That sluggish driver in front of you shouldn't really ruin your *entire* day. Often, without a therapist's prompting, a patient will conclude, "I hadn't realized how much that bothered me" or even "It's really not such a big deal now that I say it out loud." Other common reactions include "Sheesh, I sound like a spoiled brat" and "I guess I could have said that differently."

Often I'll stop a patient who feels rushed and pressured to tell me something, or I'll return to the issue to extract more details. I ask questions and encourage the patient to go over the experience one more time, recalling other aspects, observations, features, and facets. Going over the details, refining the particulars, and specifying the elements enable a person to take a logical and complete inventory of the issues or events.

Part of the therapeutic value of venting is simply giving yourself the freedom to voice your reactions about your experiences. You might spend the whole day squelching your feelings of annoyance. If you really can't let them slide off your back, then you're suppressing your anger, and this will increase your stress-hormone level. Fear and anger—whether they're intense and abrupt or mild but long-term—take a physical toll on your brain: your body tries to defend itself by producing cortisol and other hormones. At the same time, stress depletes the vitamins and amino acids in your system. When amino acid levels are reduced, the neurotransmitters that are responsible for the production of "feel-good" chemicals such as serotonin and dopamine are inhibited. Over time this will affect your appearance, your mood, your memory, and your life span.

In the early sessions of therapy, it is not unusual for venting to consume the entire time. That's because daily complaints come to mind most easily, and letting go in that fashion seems natural. Venting continues to play a role, though increasingly minor, after the patient and the therapist begin to explore thornier issues. The patient quickly learns that the first few minutes of every session offer the opportunity to put her issues out there. It's her time. Life doesn't feel so scattered when someone is listening regularly to the rehashing of the day's events. Once a patient gets used to opening up, she looks forward to spewing the boring details and the little frustrations—from all of the conversations, e-mails, or phone calls—as well as relating the full-scale tantrums and crises that make or break her day.

In fact, patients learn to "save" and store up these details in order to take them to therapy. They take comfort in knowing that they have a time and a place in which to assign an order to all of the pieces of what can sometimes feel like a chaotic or senseless existence. Venting is not the basis of therapy, but as I said earlier, it is a very important part of the process. Once patients get used to getting things off their chest, venting no longer feels like a luxury. They look forward to it. That's why venting is a vital part of this self-analysis program.

Vent to . . . Myself?

Although you might think that talking aloud to yourself would be the next best thing to talking to a therapist, writing down your thoughts is a much closer equivalent, clinically. Talking to yourself is useful when you're practicing for an interview, psyching yourself up for an important challenge, or calming yourself down after an argument. In order to legitimize your experiences as you would in therapy, however, you have to record them. This is where journal writing comes into play.

Free-associating in your journal assignments is a key component of self-analysis. Stream-of-consciousness writing is analogous to voicing or chronicling the day's events in therapy. If you write with conviction in your notebook or on your computer, you can achieve the identical goal of therapeutic venting, just as if you were sitting on a couch or a chair across from Dr. So-and-So. Every day you will write, just as you would vent in therapy, starting with the first thing from your day that comes to mind: that flash of temper when things didn't go your way or your feelings of loneliness when a phone call you expected didn't come. There is no need for punctuation, spell-check, or hesitation; just let yourself go.

To complete this part of the therapy on your own, you need to get over feeling self-conscious about what you write; you must silence the inner voice that tells you this is silly or embarrassing. When you are venting, a therapist will not censor you or be judgmental. His or her looking at you and listening will encourage you to continue to talk. Use the same principle for your journal writing.

Don't worry that writing about your fears or problems will cause them to materialize. Paying attention to your worries in this constructive way will simply make them more manageable. The idea that they'll somehow gravitate toward you more quickly, become more real, or come to fruition if you don't quickly find some wood to knock on is silly. It's true that continually whining about a problem can take up energy that you could use for positive thinking, but there is no research that shows that thinking about a tsunami, worrying about getting hit by a car, or having your child tested for a learning disability will increase the possibility of that event occurring.

The aforementioned phrase *constructive way* is the key; writing about your fears and problems in this exercise is productive—you'll see. It's not predictive, it's not foreshadowing; it's writing them down so that you can take them apart and make them solvable, or at least tolerable. Remember what I said earlier about how patients save up pieces of their week to tell their therapist? When these pieces are put down on paper, you can see them in black and white. Those feelings are no longer swirling around in your head endlessly, reminding you that you really shouldn't have done this or grilling you on why you said that.

Yes, You Are a Writer

Are you concerned about the actual process of writing? Don't be. Writing is something you do every day in one way or another, whether or not you consider yourself a poet. If you can tap out an e-mail, text-message a reminder to a friend, scribble a grocery list on a napkin or a scrap of paper, you can do this. Writing will help you to start putting things in order and to recall all that happened to you. It keeps important details from slipping or fading away.

Don't forget the rule: you are going to spend forty-five minutes a day writing, all in one session. At first you will be free-associating, then you'll write answers to questions and exercises. On some days you'll find that you can jump right into the assignments, and on other days you'll need to warm up a bit by venting.

Remember that everything is important; don't discount the bits and pieces or what seems to be pointless. Annoyances, trivial events—whatever comes to mind, put it down. You don't have to focus on the negative elements, either. Write down anything that made you grin, chuckle, or feel proud.

Keep in mind that no one is going to be reading these writings except you, so feel free to put it all down on paper. There are no limits. Nothing is irrelevant or inappropriate.

In the midst of your writing, even on this first day, you may find yourself experiencing a great sense of relief. You might start out knotted, tangled up, or simply overwhelmed, but you'll end up feeling better because you were able to compartmentalize your thoughts and feelings. This is the reason for the exercise. What is so nice about venting is that you are a free agent. You can just let it all hang out. The results—the postventing relax response and the realizations—will happen on their own.

Chronicling your thoughts and responding to questions will start the therapeutic effects automatically. It's like taking a vitamin. Go through the motions regularly, give it your all, and believe that by writing, just as by talking in therapy, you'll arrive at solutions and insights you never would have reached otherwise. You don't have to take my word for it, however; start today, and you'll see for yourself. Keep in mind that your level of commitment and motivation is directly correlated with the extent of the results.

Getting Started

Sometimes writing is hard. It feels as if you're back in school, and it's hard to trust that no one else will ever read it and criticize. After all, how often do you do something for a nonexistent audience? A song in the shower, a little dance when you are by yourself in your underwear, the "here's looking at you, kid" smile that you give yourself in the mirror—these are few and far between and don't have a therapeutic goal (aside from the benefits of a burst of momentary happiness).

You might sit in front of your journal at first, pen in hand, staring at that blank sheet of paper, and say, "She's kidding, right? I'm supposed to do this every day?" Believe me, you can. We'll start slowly. Here is a list of common questions (and answers) that can help you on your way:

Q. What if I can't think of anything to write?

A. Write about that very sense of frustration. Write about how you wish you could convey on paper what you want to say. The problem isn't that you can't write; the problem is that you've always written in a thoughtful, purposeful way, worrying about spelling and grammar, and this free-form method is completely the opposite. If you keep moving the pen, or your fingers on the keyboard, the process will become easier. Take comfort in the fact that writers throughout history have found a blank page intimidating; they too had to develop ways to fill that white space.

Journal writing is easier than trying to start a story or an essay, because you're not trying to organize your thoughts to culminate in a revelation; you're just trying to let them out. Don't try to put your thoughts in order—just start pushing your pen across the page or tapping on the keyboard. You also don't have to start at the beginning of the day and proceed chronologically to the end. Write down the thoughts that matter the most to you first. What made the strongest impression on you today? What did you say or do that you'd like to take back? You'll find that as you write, one idea will lead to another. You'll start making connections without even trying. You might even get to the point where your hand can't move as fast as your mind is dictating!

Q. My "problem" seems so generic. I keep hearing myself say, "Everyone goes through this, so stop complaining, you big baby!"

A. This time you aren't complaining. This is a legitimate step in your self-analysis plan. Be patient with yourself. There is no guide that can tell you which problems are "worthy" and which ones are not. What is mildly irritating to you might be excruciating to someone else, and vice versa. This is work, not whining.

Q. Sometimes I write something, and then I think, "That's not really true, is it?"

A. This insight is very important. Put a question mark or a star next to what you wrote. This signals the beginning of a dialogue with yourself. You're starting to question what is true, what is fluctuating, and what has moved or changed in your opinion or in your life.

Q. What if I write in my journal one day, but I read it back the next day and it makes absolutely no sense?

A. Relax. Eventually you'll be able to follow your train of thought back to where it started. Cut yourself some slack for now. This is supposed to resemble free verse. If you really feel the need for a structure, however, try to imagine that you're writing a letter to a relative or a close friend—only in this case, you are venting about the day to that relative or friend. That's not meant to be limiting; people often jump around from one topic to the next when they are writing letters. Another method of journaling that might be helpful is to write as though you're having a conversation with someone (for in a way, you are—with yourself). Write the way you would talk out loud, with incomplete sentences, with asides, with exclamation points, in whatever way allows you to get your point across. Besides, unless it's in your day's assignments, you shouldn't be looking back on your work, only forward!

Q. What if I write every day and nothing happens? What if I go through all of this effort and I don't feel any better?

A. Expect it to work. Have fun. Stop checking under the bandage. Just let the current take you where it will. Remember what I said on day 1 about not censoring yourself. Praise yourself for continuing to write, for persevering and honoring your commitment.

Q. I already know what is wrong with me (e.g., I am commitment-phobic, I binge-eat, I don't have closure). Do I still have to go through this whole process, or can I jump ahead a few chapters?

A. Think of this as physical therapy that strengthens a muscle or a tendon that is injured and helps to balance the surrounding tissue and the body parts on the other side that have been compensating. Proper alignment is not only necessary for your body; your mind needs that stability, too. So don't race; you can't jump ahead.

Q. How will I know I am doing the freewriting journal stuff correctly?

A. The process will become easier. You'll see the blank page before you for a few seconds, and the streams of thought will come sooner. You won't be bothered by sentences that fizzle or precise words you can't recall— you'll feel more natural "talking to yourself." Because you become more comfortable with the act of writing the more you write, you'll feel more relaxed at the end of the forty-five minutes than at the beginning.

Q. What if a good memory comes to me in a dream, while I'm standing in line at the supermarket, or while I'm watching a baseball game?

A. Remember the rule about carrying a pad with you at all times. Even the back of an ATM receipt will do in a pinch. You can also call yourself on the phone and leave yourself a message if you can't find any paper. Listen for the bubbling up of ideas that will happen when you start this process. You'll find that a relevant memory or thought will pop up out of nowhere. It may come in the morning or right before you doze off, in that hazy state between wakefulness and sleeping. Many of my patients have had some of their most insightful thoughts while or after exercising. Thinking that you'll remember them and write them down later, however, is one of the biggest mistakes you can make—because you won't. That bubble of a thought that pops up is important; make it standard practice to stop when the moment strikes and whip out your pen to record your observation, insight, or memory.

ASSIGNMENT

Start your free-associating, your therapeutic journaling, by answering the following questions:

1. Why?   Unless you've been in therapy, no one has probably ever asked you what you want. I'm not talking about what you want for Christmas or your birthday, or if you want fries with that shake. I'm talking about what you want for the next stage of your life, how you see yourself evolving, and what your personal goals are. Most people think that if you've made it to adulthood, have gotten a job, and have had a family, you are there—where you want to be, where you should be. Life moves so fast that you don't have time to stop and look around, survey the landscape, and assess the damage around you. The real you can easily get lost.

Your friends and neighbors aren't usually going to ask what you want out of life. We live in a world where strangers and casual acquaintances say, "How are you?" or "What's up?" without really wanting to know the answer. You probably respond in the same vein: "Fine, thanks. And you?" or "How're *you* doin'?" These people honestly don't want an answer that includes your mental state, your dreams, your frustrations, or your innermost desires. When you are feeling down, confused, distraught, or just plain sad, you might end up actually feeling worse after this type of shallow encounter day after day.

Maybe you don't have a therapist or a close friend who will ask you probing questions and really wants to hear the answers. Maybe you never gave anyone a hint that you wanted to be asked. Maybe the problem is so obvious that no one has come straight out and asked you, "You are not happy; what would make you happy?" We live in a society where even friends and family often tiptoe around a problem because it seems impolite to ask, or they simply don't want to get involved.

Your honest answer to "How are you?" might be "Not so good," "I'm tired," "I'm worried," or just a simple "Blah." If you take that moment for a time-out to actually figure out how you really are, however, you might find that your eyes fill up with tears or that you're suddenly feeling pretty bummed out. Rather than trying to distract yourself, keep sitting with that feeling for a moment. Then follow it up with a simple question: "Why?" Start to write, wherever you are. Then, during your journal session, expand on what you wrote down earlier. Keep writing the answer to "Why?" until you have spilled your guts out on the paper and are feeling drained and empty, figuratively speaking.

Again, if you're having trouble getting started, tap into the first topic that comes to mind. Writing from the inside out—starting small, with one specific incident, and expanding to record your feelings about it and then your feelings in general—can be a very useful way to explore all sorts of topics that really matter to you.

This exercise is such a challenge because being able to hear yourself think above the chatter of everyday noise is very hard. Everything in our society is set up so that people don't hear themselves, so that there is constant noise around you: the television, the radio, people talking, the sounds from the street; ticking, buzzing, beeping, ringing. You rarely sit in silence in order to listen to your breath, to try to hear the beat of your heart, to ask the hard questions. It's uncomfortable. It's easier to keep running, to keep thinking of what you have to do from your list of things to be done today. Stopping to ask how you feel means that you might have to admit or confront uncomfortable things, and who wants to do that if he or she can avoid it?

2. *Free-Associate* Look at your answer to "Why?".
Start in whatever way you can to write down every
reason you feel this way—every single one. This
includes the big reasons, the small ones, the irrelevant ones, the silly ones, and the farfetched ones.
When you free-associate in this way, the defenses
that have kept the truth at bay are more likely to
crumble. When you find yourself pausing and wondering if a certain reason deserves attention, don't
hesitate: write it down.

Every time you think you've run out of things to
write, take a deep breath and start again. Be tough on
yourself: ask yourself "And what else?" Keep going
with that fresh idea, and explore it until the well
dries up.

Another technique is to pause to ask yourself
questions (e.g., Have I felt this way before? When?
Was it a specific thing that set me off? Was I feeling
guilty or just frustrated?). Pretty soon ideas will start
bubbling up, even crowding in on you. Try to stay
focused on "Why?". Your next train of thought may
surface out of the blue. The voice you hear might
be as loud as that of the Wizard of Oz or as quiet as
Tinker Bell's. Then start writing again. Keep asking
yourself "Why?" over and over, until you feel fairly
certain that you have all the reasons in front of you.

Why does the journal method work? When you
talk in therapy, your therapist listens to your entire
winding story and then summarizes, reflects, and
interprets what you are feeling. How do you do this
for yourself? Start by acknowledging your feelings
in your writing. In a way this is like a diary, but the
process of writing in this journal is designed to teach
you to focus inward for answers.

Usually when you are searching for an answer in life, you tend to look outward. This time, however, you need to turn inward and look for the answer within yourself by doing things like freewriting. The idea of turning inward to be able to then stretch further is very Taoist. Our usual knee-jerk reaction is to do more, run faster, and look more vigilantly for signs, when what we should be doing is closing our eyes, taking a deep breath, and finding the answer exactly where it will always be: inside ourselves.

3. Advanced Work

- Write down the New Year's resolutions that you've made over the last few years. Then write down the top three "would have's, could have's, should have's."

- When you can't sleep, what is going through your head? Are there recurring scenes, or are they images of your day's activities?

- Write down any snippets of dreams. You should keep a notepad or a notebook by your bed so you can write them down immediately after waking up. Dreams fade away quickly once you wake up.

You can do this kind of venting every day to get warmed up before your assignments if you need to. Some days you'll find you can jump right into the assignment, others you'll need a nudge that this stream-of-consciousness writing can give you. Free-associating in your journal assignments is a key component of self-analyzing.

DAY THREE

So . . . Tell Me about Your Childhood

Tell me about your childhood," your therapist says. "Ha!" you think. "I knew that question was coming!" The request may not come out in such a textbook way; maybe it would be something like "Tell me about yourself: your background, growing up. Start wherever you want."

Yesterday, you wrote how you felt—unhappy, numb, fat, restless, angry—and then you went into "Why?". Maybe you concluded that you got the short end of the stick, that no one told you it would be this way, that you made some bad choices, that your family is nuts, and that life is really unfair.

So now the therapist wants to know: How did you get to this point? Which decisions and circumstances brought you to where you are today? No big painful breakthroughs are required. Think of your response in a format such as a timeline of events: date, event; date, event.

Why does telling your story—the chronology of events in your life up to the present—help? What is done is done, isn't it? That's all wrong, actually. Therapists will ask about your past if they come from a clinical background of analysis, which holds that early relationships affect adult relationships, or if they are looking for the source of your issues way back in your personal history. Cognitive-behavioral therapy, in contrast, focuses mainly on your current thoughts and on changing them. Most people, however, whether or not they are expecting the "Tell me about your childhood" statement, already know that their patterns come from very young interactions, and they want to talk about their past.

Pulling together the puzzle pieces of your life experience in order to create the big picture of who you are today is something you may never have attempted before with this much deliberation. You certainly have people around you who know about certain years of your life in detail—your best friend from high school knows everyone you had a crush on, and your sister remembers all of your childhood injuries—but no one has been with you on the long road of your life day after day and stood at your side at every crossroad. No one has, in fact, seen the epic movie or read the entire *War and Peace*–sized memoir of your life that explains how you think and act today.

Your story includes years and years of growing up, of positive and negative interactions with parents and other family members, of friendships made and broken, of jobs held or aspired to, of dreams and illusions embraced or discarded.

Your verbal memoir is multifaceted, made up of numerous story lines and perspectives, and your therapist has the remarkable ability to keep track of them simultaneously.

There is more, however: your narrative also has visuals and emotions, which may range from awkward to colorful. The therapist keeps them from twisting and tangling, as if they were marionette strings, thereby allowing you to continue effortlessly with your stream of thought. Being able to look back and verbally paint a longitudinal picture of your perspective of an event at the age you were when it happened, interjected with your present view, will result in the longest story you've ever told.

Hence the therapist becomes the guardian of your life story. The realization that someone has the real and entire version of your life, past and present, a complicated amalgam that explains how you got to be the person you are today, is extraordinarily liberating. It gives you a solid therapeutic base from which to start questioning and looking to change your reality. You are protected and guided and can move forward uncensored. There is no right or wrong answer; there is no exam at the end of the session.

Once you start articulating your story in this context, a new way of telling it evolves. You have the luxury of being long-winded and circuitous. Every byway or alley you may wander down is mapped and noted. You may stop halfway through a sentence because some other thought has become more pressing, or a memory totters in, interrupting for a moment. You don't have to follow a set chronological timeline; you can jump ahead ten years without a poetic transition. If a thought pops into your head, you can come to an inelegant, screeching halt and veer off in another direction. You don't have to worry: the therapist keeps track of everything and holds on to it for you.

During venting, most patients slip readily into talking about their past and their experiences growing up. It might come naturally when you ask yourself why things don't feel right. You may find yourself listing factors and saying something like "I always feel responsible; you see, in my family I was the oldest and I had to look out for my siblings" or "Telling the exact truth is very important to me. When I was growing up, my parents often exaggerated or minimized, and it was something that really bothered me."

If a patient has trouble leaping from the present to the past and back again, a therapist may nudge him or her by asking questions: "When have you thought that way before?" "Where did that idea come from?" "Who around you agreed or disagreed?" Just like a friend who reminds you where you were in your story before you were interrupted, a therapist facilitates the flow so that you can easily pick up the thread again and continue weaving in and out of different time frames.

Most people find that as they start telling their life story for the first time in this gentle, unrushed way, they start to remember more and more features and details. Events and people they hadn't thought about in years suddenly appear in their dreams. This time, however, there is a therapeutic collage into which they can paste them and then add other images, words, and sentences that collectively describe a past.

Once you start, the therapist seems like a transcriber to you for this part of the process. He or she doesn't usually interject at this point, other than to ask you to clarify or expand, but simply becomes a reporter who is, in a sense, writing your biography.

Just as would happen in therapy, the story you write about yourself might flow sequentially from venting, or it might come out in dribs and drabs within the free-associating you are learning to do. Either way is fine. As long as it's down on paper, your brain and your soul will start moving into this process naturally. Memories will float up that connect events and people. Your job is to listen to them, make sure that you catch them, and write them down.

Your Side of the Story

This isn't your mom's version of your accomplishments when she's gushing to a neighbor about you. It's not a blurb from your high school yearbook or the essay from your college application. This is a raw, uncut, director's version with explicit adult language, bloopers, footage never seen before, and full-frontal nudity. In short, it is embarrassing at times, boring at others, and unrivaled, as far as you're concerned. It is your story, whether you want to start it by remembering your room as an infant looking through the slats of your crib or by admitting who really started the fights in the backseat of the car.

What will happen organically in both day 1 and day 2 of therapy (or however long these venting and chronicling topics take in real-time therapy) is that the benefits will appear with minimal effort on your part. Just as you don't feel the fiber from whole-grain bread cleansing your colon, and you don't feel a vitamin supplement boosting your immune system, you won't feel seismic psychological tremors rumbling, but without a doubt a stage is being set for the story of your life. Keep in mind, then, some of these benefits:

- Telling the story in therapy creates a place, a haven, where you can tell the truth about absolutely everything. No one will call human resources, your grandmother, or the press. Your story is safe and in one place: your literary "vault."

- Telling the story will make you automatically question what happened at each crossroad. When was the last time you were able to revisit a decision from ten years ago? How does it feel today? Is it more glaringly obvious now that it was the wrong choice, or have the corners smoothed out and it's become more bearable?

- Telling the story will make you comprehend how little control you had over your life when you were a child and an adolescent. All too often, as an adult, you forget that most of the things that happened to you when you were a child were not your fault. Who in your family drank and what happened when they did, how often your parents fought and why, where you moved to, or whom you had to sit next to— seldom were you asked your opinion. It all pretty much happened *to* you, and you had to roll with the punches.

- Telling the story will make you realize that the makeup of your family was not your choice. You didn't choose your father—your mother did (whether or not she was trying to get pregnant). As you start describing your family at different stages of your life, you might be surprised at the harsh but appropriate descriptions you use. Did you ever wonder if you were dropped off in a basket on the front steps? If so, do you wish that the person who left you had picked the neighbors instead? Have you ever hoped that you were adopted? Have you waited impatiently for the alien spaceship to beam you back up? You aren't alone.

- Telling the story will make you see when certain patterns of behavior began. Adding approximate or specific dates helps to clarify and define the timeline. You didn't always think as you do now: there was a before, and there will be an after.

- Telling the story will illuminate how you came to define yourself as "the smart aleck," "the nice girl," or "the ugly one." Did one touchdown in a football game in high school make you a winner for that year and give you a formative experience in your definition of you? Did your taller twin brand you "the short one" and destine you to be Napoleonic in your career choices? Have you settled into talking about glory days since college, or do you cringe at every reunion because you'll have to hear a dreaded nickname? How has your definition of yourself changed, and what remains true?

- Telling the story will help you to remember things you had forgotten. You'll catch yourself saying, "I don't remember much about junior high school," then you'll find that memories slowly start to fill in what you thought was a year or a decade of insignificant, hazy recollections of your favorite junk food or commercial jingle.

- Telling the story will help you to question situations and recognize that you may have misunderstood quite a few of them. What you experienced when you were a child or as an adolescent was colored by how much you overheard or intuited. (Many parents underestimate how much children know about family discord.) For a child, the time a situation lasted may have felt infinitely long. Finding out how long it was in reality can help you to make sense of things.

- Telling the story will help you to start coming to terms with people you haven't forgiven. Don't worry,

I'm not asking you to forgive them. Just acknowledging that you haven't will allow you to lay all your cards on the table. How long have you held these grudges? Did these people hurt your feelings or those of someone you loved? Do they even know that you still scorn them? Are there any other resolutions besides outright forgiveness or continued contempt?

- Telling the story will help you to clarify how you got to where you find yourself now. Although patients are logical, functioning, and intelligent human beings, so many come into therapy trying to understand "How did I get on this merry-go-round, and how do I get off?" By detailing events on a continuum, they can start to understand the events and dynamics that incrementally (or drastically) influenced the paths they took, instead of feeling shipwrecked on a godforsaken island.

You can start this process automatically by just starting to talk about yourself—on paper.

Where Do I Start?

If after venting you don't feel compelled to talk about the past, you might like to start at the very beginning—the very, very beginning. Go back to the first event you recall. Even if the memories are fuzzy, hang onto them and put them down on paper. Then move on to the next moment of recall. The story will expand as you include what you thought were the perspectives of others. You might jump ahead, then, and describe how you realized you were right, wrong, or oblivious when, ten years later, your tipsy uncle divulged a family secret during the annual barbecue. As a plot unfolds in a movie, you'll tell the story through the eyes of a child (when you were eight, nine, or fourteen), then switch to "What I didn't know," "What my father didn't tell me," and so on. Then you can zigzag to where you left off on that tangent, at age ten or fifteen, and continue.

Perhaps penning the first line seems as daunting as deciding on a tattoo, your first baby's name, or an inscription on a tombstone. Where you start is not a big deal. Here are a few opening lines that others have used to get things rolling:

> Maycomb was a tired old town, even in 1932 when I first knew it. Somehow, it was hotter then.
>
> —Harper Lee, *To Kill a Mockingbird*

> It started—for me, it started—last Thursday, in response to an urgent message from my nurse. I hurried home from a medical convention I'd been attending.
>
> —Jack Finney, *The Body Snatchers*

> Many years later when he faced the firing squad, Colonel Aureliano Buendia was to remember that distant afternoon when his father took him to discover ice.
>
> —Gabríel García Márquez, *One Hundred Years of Solitude*

Keep in mind that your opening sentence need not be memorable or even original. Just start.

ASSIGNMENT

To write about your past, you can either just start writing, as fast and as much as you can, or you can use the following questions. If you run out of things to write about on your own, come back to these questions and make sure you've addressed all of them.

1. Chronicle a history of your body. What was the first injury you remember? Take an inventory of the scars on your body. How did you get each one?

2. Review your vocational history. How did you answer, when you were a child, when you were asked what you wanted to be? Did you get an allowance? What was your first job? Remember when you had to update your résumé. What careers did you think about? What pushed or pulled you in one direction or another? If you could work at anything you wanted now, what would it be? What would you do if you won the lottery? When do you want to retire, and what do you want to do then?

3. Tell your spiritual or religious history. What do you remember thinking about God when you were little? How did your views seem different from those of others, or did most people around you have similar ideas? Do you remember being puzzled about or angry at God?

4. Take an inventory of your relationship history. What was the first word you uttered? Was it "Mama," "Papa," or "cookie"? Who was your first best friend? What was your first sexual experience like? Who are the main people in your network now?

If you're still having difficulty, try answering the following brief questions in just one or two sentences. Then go back to the preceding questions and give them another try:

- Which years of your childhood memories are fuzzy?
- Are there stories you've been told so often that you consider them yours?
- What stories about you do you know that your family has exaggerated?
- What parenting styles did your parents use in raising you?
- When you look at pictures of yourself as a child, what do you think of that little person?
- When did you feel invincible? When did it seem as if you had reached a plateau or gotten a reality check from the world?
- What songs are stuck in your head from years ago? Which scenes from movies run through your mind?
- In what ways was your childhood or adolescence different from that of your friends?
- Did you ever get caught doing something that shamed you? How did your parents deal with it?
- What moments do you wish you could remember more vividly?

Other Helpful Prompts

Are you still having a rough time getting started? Do you keep hitting ruts? Don't despair: start with one of the following sentences or ideas, and keep adding details until you run out of things to say, then go on to the next:

- "I can't help the way I am—look at what I had to grow up with!" (Now write what that "what I had to grow up with" was.)

- "I've always been this way, even when I was a little kid." (What is "this way"?)

- "I'm too hard on myself" (or "I take things too personally," "I obsess," "I am lazy," "I am a dreamer," "I am high-strung," "I have no sense of humor," "I am too nice"). Write down at least one of the things you have heard about yourself at different times in your life—when you were a child or an adolescent, as stated by a teacher, a coach, a family member, or a lover—and keep writing.

- "I was a sweet baby," "I was a real brat," "I started to talk when I was six months old," "I was always stubborn." Choose one that you think is true, and start expanding on it. Even if you have to describe yourself as an infant, you can do it. Your own recollection may be pretty sketchy, but you've been hearing your baby stories forever—either as whispers between adults or comments to you as you looked at photo albums. Do you agree with how people described you?

- "My chin is too pointy," "I'm too fat," "My arms are so long." Are any of these you? If not, think of what a caricature of you would look like if someone drew a cartoon of you and exaggerated all of your features. Choose one feature. You'll cringe, maybe; it can be embarrassing, but don't let that stop you.

Is this all too serious? Are you feeling a bit overwhelmed? Maybe lightening up would help. Try having a bit of fun with the following:

- If you were allowed to pick a characteristic or a superpower, what would it be?

- In which movie would you choose to play the main character?

- If you won a million dollars, what would you do with it?

- If you found a genie lamp, what would your wishes be?

- You are about to perform in front of a crowd in some way or to play a decisive tennis match. What is your inspiration song?

- This Halloween you have to dress up, and the sky is the limit. Who or what would you be?

- How do you psych yourself up? (It could be for a tennis match, for a presentation, or just to get up and drag yourself to work.) Maybe you say to yourself, "I can bash my opponent and crush him in the palm of my hand!" or perhaps, "I might not be as strong physically, but mentally I am tough as nails!"

A Few More Tips

Here are some handy tips to use while you are writing:

- Use a thesaurus. It's not cheating; go ahead.

- Don't forget to mention birth order.

- Play music from your childhood; it's a surefire way to bring up memories.

Whew! If you've made it this far, you're doing great. Day 1 was difficult—making the commitment. Day 2 was the beginning of the serious work. Now that you have actually started telling your story, you have just passed the 20 percent mark—and believe it or not, that means that the end is in sight.

Telling your story provides you with the ammunition to shoot down all of your old fears, get rid of the skeletons rattling around in the closet of your head, and dump that weighty mental garbage can you've been hauling around.

Q and A

Q. I don't get the idea of memories "popping" into my head. Do you have any other description that might make more sense to me?

A. One of my patients was not convinced of the bubbling up analogy, either, and said, "For me it's more like something flits across the screen in my mind or runs across like a streaker at an English soccer game." It's very personal.

Q. Chronicling my life feels sort of like going to confession. Is that weird?

A. Not at all. I know that it can bring up feelings of guilt, shame, and repentance, and, finally, of forgiveness. As long as you have a range of feelings and you are noting them, as well, you are on the right track.

Q. Telling my story is such a daunting request. Is it that important? Can it really give you that much information?

A. Telling your story is so important that Sir William Osler, who has been called the father of modern medicine, taught his students at the turn of the twentieth century that the patient's story will often contain the key to making a diagnosis. "Listen carefully to the patient," Osler advised his students. "They will tell you the diagnosis." Even now, 75 percent of medical diagnoses are based on the patient's story alone. In addition, so much healing comes from telling your story that it is the basis for much of the work done by Eve Ensler, the creator of *The Vagina Monologues*.

Q. Isn't it important to make sure that your memories are based on reality?

A. Actually, memories are in some sense more important than the reality. How you perceive things *is* your reality. Some of the most important parts of your story will be precisely about your very personal experience. Regardless of your family's income, did you feel rich or poor? Regardless of how many siblings you had, did you feel ostracized and lonely?

Q. It's amazing how certain songs bring back memories! Who else has written about this?

A. One of my favorite authors, the neurologist Oliver Sacks, describes in his book *Musicophilia* how music has the magical quality of being attached to unconscious memories.

Q. To write about my spiritual history, you mention times of being puzzled about or angry at God. Do you mean the one in which my family wanted me to believe? The one to whom most of the people around me prayed?

A. I mean whoever was the higher power for you at that time. Granted, people's definitions of that can change. When I say God, I mean God with a big *G* or a small *g*, Mother Earth, Jesus Christ, Krishna, the universe—whoever or whatever works for you.

DAY FOUR

Fantasy and Feedback

Today we're going to start with an exercise that requires a response from others. You'll be using their answers in tomorrow's assignment. You'll need their responses by tomorrow morning, so there's no time to lose.

Few people ever ask for honest feedback about themselves, so don't expect your family or friends to understand this request right away—or even to be eager to participate. You simply want feedback about how others experience you. So, as much as you'd like to just guess or assume, you are going to be asking people who know you for this information. Don't freak out; I'll explain. It's not as bad as it sounds.

First, whom should you choose to ask? Think about the people who care about you and who would support you

on this self-improvement quest. Think of people you can
trust to be candid. Also consider the best communicators:
individuals who you know will devote the time and the
energy to detail a response for you, not just tell you that
you are, of course, fabulous and gloss over the importance
of this exercise.

Take time to explain to them that this is a way of
helping you and that you really want and need their
opinions—no matter what the opinions are. Don't expect
that the people who know and love you will always be
honest. After all, they don't want to hurt your feelings.
If you're lucky, a few friends will tell you exactly what
they're thinking and give you some useful constructive
criticism.

More likely, however, they'll be inclined to tell you what
they believe you want to hear—not what they actually
think. So encourage them to be honest and stress more
than once that you won't be upset if they say something
that seems negative. Emphasize that you want and need
their help and that this exercise is aimed at just one thing:
helping you to get a better, more accurate picture of how
the world experiences you.

Write an e-mail to seven people whom you've identified as good candidates. You can copy the template below
or write your own version, if you prefer. If you do rewrite
it, make sure that you retain the key points.

Dear XXX,

As part of a self-help program I am completing, I have to ask those who know me well to
give me some feedback about myself. Please
answer the following questions as honestly and

openly as possible. Since this is part of a program, please respond by 9 a.m. tomorrow. I
sincerely appreciate it and thank you for your
feedback.

1. How would you describe me to someone you
   wanted to set me up with on a blind date?
2. How would you describe me to a potential
   employer?
3. What are some good traits that I have but
   don't seem to be aware of?
4. Most important, what are some negative
   characteristics that I should work on?

I realize that answering question 4 might make
you a little uncomfortable, but please be assured
that I won't interpret your comments as criticism of me as a person. I will receive them as
helpful observations that will provide me with
an opportunity to become aware of behavior
patterns of which I may be oblivious. I'm asking several people the same questions, so don't
worry, you won't be the only source.

Again, thanks for your help. I look forward to
hearing from you.

When you have sent the e-mails, call the recipients to
let them know that there is an important e-mail in their
inboxes. If they try to drag more details out of you, don't
engage them. Limit yourself to telling them that you're in
a self-help program that requires you to ask for feedback
from people close to you. Tell them that you've asked
them four simple questions, and that everything will be
clear once they've read the e-mail.

Fantasy and Reality

Okay, we now return to our regularly scheduled program.

At this point in therapy, your therapist would move from asking questions about your background or your daily life to asking about how you would like your life to be, what is the best-case scenario for your future, what is on your wish list, and what your aspirations are. In other words, whereas yesterday's exercise was focused on your history—dates, events, and your perception of those events—today we are going to consider the future and the topic of your hopes and dreams. In short, we are going to look at who you would like to be.

As you detail how you've experienced life and what your wishes are, your therapist would be piecing together the bigger picture of how others experience you. You would talk about your friendships and might even consider bringing a family member in to therapy with you. You could be recommended for group therapy, in which the participants give feedback to one another—sometimes in harsh and direct ways, sometimes more politely.

The purpose of this is to get some solid facts about how you affect those around you and whether the way you see yourself in your mind's eye is accurate. You could be in for a rude awakening, you could be relieved, or you could find that deep down inside, you knew you weren't fooling anyone. You might, nonetheless, be surprised to discover that you have been way too harsh on yourself.

Thus, the second topic today (after who you would like to be) is how you are seen by others and how you think you appear to others—both the good and the bad. This is a variation of couples or family therapy, group therapy, and social skills training. Everyone, no matter how perfect, can use a little brushing up on social etiquette and learn to take praise along with constructive criticism.

The Ideal You

To get information on the first you—the one you wish you were—your therapist might pause and ask, "How would you have wanted that event to play out?" You might also be asked to paint a picture of an alternative ending to a story you have told. What if you could go back in time and marry your childhood sweetheart? What if you had made that other decision, taken that other job, or said yes instead of no to that offer? What if you had taken the low road instead of the high road, run off with a lover, or joined the traveling circus, the marines, a cult, or a band?

If you rewrote your story so that you were enjoying the perfect ending today and absolute happiness was yours, how much of the rewrite would feature vindictive fantasies? Maybe you'd get your mother to admit that she was wrong, you'd inspire awe in those who considered you mediocre, or you'd go back and kick the bully.

We all have these fantasies, but we don't turn into spiteful people unless we act on them. The key is to bring them into awareness, and this is what the writing exercises in this book help you to do. Once the fantasies are on the page, externalized, you can look at them in an objective way and thus prevent them from exercising power over you so that you don't wallow in self-pity and what could have been (or live in what the writer James Thurber called the "basement of the pluperfect subjunctive").

One of the principles of psychoanalysis is that whatever you become conscious of, you can control. When you become aware of what you wish had happened in your life or of the person you wish you could have been, you can take the first step toward re-creating the life that you truly want. By getting in touch with your deepest impulses and motivations, you gain the ability to think of creative, constructive ways of manifesting them. Mourn fully so you can start healing; understand your unfulfilled fantasy so you can stop regretting. Wishful thinking renders you powerless.

The insight you get in therapy should help you to understand and pinpoint what you truly desire. Is it realistic? Where did that desire originate? Was it an immature reaction for revenge? Was it magical thinking that keeps you stuck throwing tantrums like a child? Or did it come from free will and an honest desire to be authentic and whole?

ASSIGNMENT

You've never picked up a guitar and you can't hold a tune when the shower isn't running, yet you wish you were a rock star. Write that down, go into the details, and try to pin down what it is you're truly yearning for. Perhaps you're in a dead-end nine-to-five job and what you really want is to free your creative spirit. If this is the case, how can you do this? Maybe you can get together with your friends in the garage and bang out some tunes that make the neighborhood dogs howl. Or does the fantasy about becoming a musician have more to do with a feeling that you went right from child to responsible adult without being able to dabble and see what you were good at doing?

What, exactly, are your talents? What small steps can you take today that will begin the process of allowing you to discover your gifts and aptitudes in a decade or two? Perhaps you're a corporate accountant but know in your heart that your strength is working with people, not numbers. Is there some volunteer work you could do that would nurture this "people" part of you? Or are you ready to take a leap and go back to school to retrain for a new career? Does it have to be all or nothing? Does exploring this frighten you because your wrong choice will become even more evident?

Read the following prompts and choose those that resonate with you. Then write as much as you can— get wild and crazy. Tap into your most deeply hidden wishes and remember that this is for your eyes only, so you can be as off-the-wall as you want.

- Consider the events you wrote about in the last chapter's exercise. How do you wish the outcomes had been different?

- Think of the crossroads in your life. What regrets do you have over taking a wrong turn, and what decisions would you have made differently?

- If money and time were not issues, how would you want to change?

- Write a wish list for your ideal self-definition. Who would you like to be? ("This is who I am; who would I like to be? How would I like to be different?")

- If you were able to change anything, even your height or your hairline, what would you change?

- Consider more complex changes. Would you want to be more trusting? Would you like to experience the world as a more optimistic place? Do you wish you could be more tolerant or more forgiving?

If nothing is coming up for you yet and you need something a little more provocative to jolt yourself into action, copy one of the following opening lines and then keep on writing. Don't stop and think; just write the first thoughts that come to mind, regardless of how bizarre or outlandish they seem. When you're sure you've written everything that's in your heart, choose another opening line.

- Physically, I wish my body were . . .
- Spiritually, I wish I were . . .
- As far as money and finances are concerned, I'd like . . .
- I think people don't like me because . . .
- I feel most misunderstood when . . .

Feedback

Although therapy is about how you feel inside, and you'd like to think of yourself as strong, solid, and imperturbable—a rock or an island—you can't live without interacting with others. Their reactions to you can affect you for an hour, for a day, or for your life. At this point (which would be months into your therapy, because this program is accelerated) your therapist might endeavor to obtain information about how you are seen by the outside world. This is a complicated process. We all crave acceptance by coworkers and friends who, despite our flaws, will still describe us as funny, generous, and just downright cool. What would happen if you actually heard their thoughts about you? What if you were in a restroom stall and two people were washing their hands and talking about you, unaware that you were just a few feet away? Are you prepared to hear that kind of uncensored opinion—the type you get when your critics feel free to speak their minds?

It might be painful to solicit information about yourself from others, but you need to make a realistic appraisal of yourself if you want to gain insight. How much does your description of yourself line up with how others experience you? You might have a friend who thinks he is quite a ladies' man, but in reality he's as slick as sandpaper, and you waffle between pity and embarrassment when you go out with him. Then there is the opposite situation: the friend who underestimates how well liked she is, how attractive she is, and how generous she is—she's completely clueless and self-deprecating.

When people look at you, what do they see? Have you ever wondered who will come to your funeral and what they will say? Would you be surprised, disappointed, or touched by how much you affected them? Would you be annoyed at how far removed their descriptions of you are from your self-image?

Television reality shows depend on the surprise that contestants feel when they hear the naked truth, either from costars talking about them or significant others recalling the same story from a different perspective. How would it be for someone to tell a friend who thinks he is funny that he's not? How would it be to shoot down a friend who thinks she is really smart but doesn't actually know any facts?

How often have you fantasized nicely, or not so nicely, about giving certain people honest feedback on how they act? Here are some examples:

- "You think you are so smart, but I already thought of that same thing ages ago."

- "I wish you'd stop that stupid, obnoxiously loud laugh; it's embarrassing."
- "You think I don't notice that you always 'forget your wallet' when we go out, but I do."
- "You think you are such a tough guy; everyone can see it's all bravado. You're not fooling anyone."
- "Enough with being the good girl already; live a little."
- "Stop with the constant apologizing."

Finally, there's the plain and simple "It's not all about you—really."

Feedback comes in all shapes and sizes. During adolescence, it may have been brutally blunt, or it may have been subtle, nonverbal social cues that would give you vital feedback if you knew how to read them. Indeed, the ability to read these cues was a critical skill that determined whether a teenager was popular or an outcast in the social hierarchy.

The same is true in adult life. When your partner is mad at you and reels off a litany of "home truths" about you, the meaning is usually made clear. It can sometimes be excruciating to listen to your annual review at work. If you have children, you've probably already discovered that they don't mince words when they tell you what they think.

Most often, the feedback you are offered is subtle, and you might find that you have chosen not to hear it for some reason: to protect your ego from bruising, because you're too lazy to change, because you're in denial about the long-term repercussions, or because you're brushing it off as others projecting their own concerns onto you. It's time to shake things up a bit; you've been stagnant for too long.

ASSIGNMENT

Think about your experience with getting feedback in life and then write down your thoughts as fully as you can. When was the last time you were told something about yourself that surprised you? Are you the type whose feelings are hurt by criticism or who brushes off negative feedback as someone else's subjective perspective? More important, when was the last time you asked for feedback? It was probably very long ago. It's much easier to find reasons not to ask.

When you do receive feedback, euphemisms are frequently used: "You get a little boisterous when you drink" (read: You get sloppy drunk and are embarrassing); "You have a strong personality" (read: It's all about you, you, you all the time; you need and demand a lot of attention). Does "You are the life and soul of the party" imply that you are entertaining but never ask others about themselves? Do you seldom, if ever, share the spotlight?

ASSIGNMENT

How often have you considered asking someone you went out on a date with to tell you about the impression you made? People seldom do, although this is the perfect person to ask: he or she noticed everything from your gait to your voice pitch. A safer, more realistic request is to ask someone you once dated who—either quickly or eventually—became a friend. Get used to the idea of getting feedback that you don't have to refute. Be careful that you don't get defensive. Remind yourself that this is about getting information from the impressions you give, which are mostly unconscious and are patterns that you have the power to change or adjust.

A Final Recommendation

Do *not* read the e-mails as they come in. Read them all together tomorrow. Resist the temptation. You have to be in the right frame of mind, and the collective reading will give you a more complete picture of the perceptions that others have of you.

Q and A

Q. I've been asked to give someone feedback who is doing this therapy work. How do I tell him or her things that are not positive? It's so uncomfortable.

A. Use whatever euphemisms or metaphors you want. Give these people a way to save face by prefacing what you write with "This is really just a detail" or something along those lines. It's up to the person to make the translation and summarize the information. He or she has the responsibility to take what you say seriously, and you should have the ability to tell this person discreetly in order to protect the friendship. Keep in mind that you won't be the only one; six others will be asked as well.

Q. How does a person develop a realistic, healthy sense of self and self-esteem?

A. Children develop a sense of self from how they master their environment, what kind of feedback they get about their skills, and how they see their parents and other caregivers treated.

Q. I asked a cousin to give me this feedback, and he asked for examples. What do I say?

A. You can give examples like the following: "Tell me how I hide behind having to take care of others at the expense of taking care of myself. Tell me that I talk too much and need to pay more attention. Tell me that I need to be friendlier in groups of people so I don't come off as arrogant. Tell me that I should ask questions about others rather than talk about myself. Tell me I play the victim too much. Tell me I, like, say *like* too often. Tell me that my reluctance to make fixed plans doesn't make me seem busy, just flaky and self-centered. Tell me that I talk too much about money. Tell me that I am sometimes condescending. Tell me that the occasional slice of humble pie would be good for me. Tell me that I need to complain less. Tell me I should take more time to listen."

Q. Can I really invite my family members to come to therapy?

A. Yes, and they will often talk about you in front of you. Somehow the dynamic of making a declaration with a third person there to observe makes the statement more meaningful, even if it was something they have said in the past. They mention good qualities and that they love you, but then they spew the bitter truth. As a therapist, I never cease to be amazed by how two people living together for ages can say things in one session that they've never heard from each other.

DAY FIVE

You've Got Mail

I hope you have withstood the temptation to read the e-mails as they came in yesterday and today. Maybe you are annoyed at the one person who still hasn't answered or the friend who has decided to make this letter a way to thank you for all you've done rather than give you the feedback you really need in order to understand yourself better and make changes. Cut them some slack—and get moving with what you have.

You are probably hesitant right now. You want to hear the good stuff, but you are anxious about the bad. Adjust your mind-set. There will be praise that you'll enjoy hearing. Many people want to balance their feedback by adding some acclaim to the constructive criticism. You probably remember a report card or an evaluation from school that tried to soften the blow by saying that you played well with others or that stressed what "character" you added to the classroom. You always "brought a different view" to the table (read: were totally off in left field) and had a "contagious enthusiasm" (read: incited everyone around you to be impulsive and loud, too).

Don't let yourself be distracted by it. You might be told that you "have a great heart" or that people can always "count on you when the going gets rough." That's nice for a toast at your birthday or your wedding, but it's not that helpful for what we are trying to do here. I want your brain to stay in practical problem-solving mode for this exercise.

However you get feedback, put aside the way that people are telling you things. They may couch their opinions with humor or try to soften their responses somehow. They may come across as very practical or add something mollifying at the end, such as "But that is the way you are, my friend, and I wouldn't have it any other way" or "But I love you, man; don't change a thing." Of course, this kind of sugarcoating is meant to be kind, but you're on the path to self-understanding and you need to be ruthless. Discard the fluff and delve into the true message.

What are your correspondents really saying to you? Do any of the e-mails share a common theme? It's the parts of you that are not so glamorous, the parts that perhaps you're ashamed of, that have to be brought into the light of day. The aim of this exercise is not to beat yourself up but to allow you to get to the bottom and shake things up, then spend as much time bettering yourself as you would your lawn or your golf swing. So if your friends and family tell you some "home truths," be excited. This is good information.

In group therapy, the feedback is sometimes vicious—the people there do not care if you ever talk to them again. In individual therapy, you get this feedback in a more gentle way through the therapist's carefully chosen questions, which make the information feel less like a slap in the face and more like an option you discovered by yourself. So rather than getting your knickers in a knot if your evaluation isn't stellar, consider yourself lucky and be grateful that the people who know you will approach this level of candidness.

The alternative is to be clueless about your blind spots, to spend your entire life walking around not knowing that you're trailing emotional toilet paper stuck to your shoe because no one has ever pointed it out to you. Perhaps you'd like a more enthusiastic response from people when you enter a room, and you have no inkling that you exude a slight (or not-so-slight) air of conceit that pushes people away. Maybe you're an inveterate people pleaser and don't realize that while you see yourself as flexible and accommodating, others view you as inauthentic or even spineless. You are doing this because you want an overhaul or a tune-up, right?

It might be painful to learn how others experience you, and it can be grueling when you start to figure out how you became that way, but bringing this material into consciousness is the key to change—and change is good.

Usually, the initial reaction to bad feedback is to be defensive. You say, "No, I'm not like that at all," or "Ugh, they just don't understand," or "Well, screw him if he thinks I am like that, I don't need his friendship, anyway," or the classic "She's just jealous." This is exactly the kind of attitude you can't afford to assume here. Sure, they like you, and having weighed the good and the bad, they still want to hang out with you. They're your friends or your relatives, and it's natural for them to speak kindly to (and of) you, but don't you want to know the gritty stuff that they think but never tell you? After all, that's where you'll find the fuel for your growth.

ASSIGNMENT

Work through all of the information you have received and identify any themes. Look at all of the feedback together, not one item by one, because who sent it is irrelevant. Try to think of it as appearing in the form of folded-up scraps of paper that you are picking out of a hat. Someone you like, and who likes you, wrote it—that's all you need to know. Mentally spread the papers out around you. Now you get to be the proverbial fly on the wall, a hidden camera that keeps playing when you leave the room. This might be one of the most important lessons you will ever have to understand: how you appear to others.

How does this new information fit into the scheme of how you see yourself? Remember how you defined yourself on day 2, and think about how the feedback you received relates to what you wrote about yourself. Can you connect the two in some way? The point of this exercise is to learn how to become a better person. You're not seeking to be better liked, necessarily; you're discovering how to flex the muscles in your personality and your psyche that you haven't used before and maybe didn't even know you had. They can instigate improvement and positive change.

Sift through the feedback and see how it fits with the image you have of yourself. See which of the following statements resonate with you; this is the kind of feedback you want. Pick out a few from this list and add others to it:

- You are generous to a fault and, in fact, are often a sucker.

- You are competitive, but sometimes you cross the line and become a sore loser.

- You are cooperative but can be perceived as a people pleaser.

- You are proud of being a good parent, but you actually dote too much on your child.

- You are pessimistic and need to get some perspective.

- You use too much hyperbole; who can believe you when you are always talking in extremes?

- You aren't stupid, but you act like an airhead sometimes.

- You like to take charge but at times come across as bossy.

- You are a terrible listener. Friends often have to repeat details of things they've told you, and they think you're not interested. Instead of listening to others, you offer your unsolicited opinion on how they need to change their lives.

- You are a hypocrite because you preach to your friends when your own life is a mess.

- You are neurotic (not sensitive). You are always having emotional meltdowns and needing help, but if anyone else has a breakdown, you run for the hills.

- You are a killjoy.

- You ask others about themselves but then don't allow them a chance to answer.

- You are not gregarious, and your friends wish you made more of an effort to talk to people around you.

- You appear close-minded and always dismiss the opinions of others.

- Your holier-than-thou attitude is irritating. It makes others feel guilty about how they live.

- You come across as conceited.

- You are way too intense; not everyone wants to be around that high energy all the time.

- You constantly act the intellectual; you really need to lighten up and learn to consider new information.

Add to this list other revelations about yourself. Write down everything that comes to mind as you work through this exercise without editing or censoring. What are the contradictions between what you think of yourself and what others think? ("I'm not bossy, I just like to take charge; I'm not a sore loser, I'm simply competitive; I'm not neurotic, I'm just sensitive") Do they ring any bells? Have you heard variations on any of these themes before?

Don't Shoot the Messenger

The key to understanding yourself is the way you react to the responses from your friends and relatives. How do they make you feel? If something someone says makes you feel sad or actually has you jumping out of your chair and screaming, "That's not true!" there is a reason it is affecting you so strongly. You will use this feedback as a starting point for deeper self-exploration.

You may find that the feedback elicits alarmingly strong feelings. This is natural. After all, in daily life you rarely get uncensored feedback of this kind. You may receive individual criticisms from time to time (which you can defend yourself against by saying things like "Well, that is only one person's opinion"), but at no time are you pelted with critical comments, many of which may reinforce one another. Note your reactions. "Ouch. Hey! Really?" "No way. That only happened once." "He doesn't really know me well, anyway." "Oh, come on!" "Yeah, well, he's right, I am that way, and hey, I like it." "I've never done that! What is she talking about? She's nuts."

Defensive rejection of the comments will only serve to keep you stuck in your old patterns. Treat the feedback as you would if you asked someone to proofread an important letter before sending it, and he or she pointed out that you were using a word incorrectly. You'd be happy that it was spotted before the letter reached its destination. This is the right attitude.

Perhaps you once tried on an article of clothing in a store and thought you looked great in it, but maybe it was just a wee tight, and when a friend said, "Uh, no, that isn't really working for you," you realized that you were indeed fooling yourself. Maybe you once had an argument with a buddy, and when you told the story to your wife, she shrugged and agreed with him: "Hmm, but babe, you kinda were out of line." So now, even if the feedback touches a raw nerve, you should be thinking, "How can I use this information to my advantage?"

Recall when you were privy to someone's opinion of you—any detail will do. It may have been delivered in a cruel way or a kind way, or it might have been merely serendipitous. Perhaps you overheard an acquaintance saying that you had bad breath, a colleague observing that you're always late, or a friend commenting that you are overly dramatic. How did you react?

Looking back and taking advantage of the benefit of time, which reduces the emotional charge, can you see how the information could have been of value to you, even though at the time you wanted to shoot or ignore the messenger? Maybe you even started carrying mints in your pocket, setting your clock five minutes fast, or being pickier about what to get overly emotional about. Learn and make a resolution that from now on, you'll extract the worthwhile information from feedback without delay or excuses, without having to wait until your ego stops throwing a tantrum.

This is indeed hard work—damn hard. Don't kid yourself. You may have grown up with the "sticks and stones can break my bones, but words will never hurt me" philosophy, but when has that ever really been true for you? Don't words have a tremendous power to hurt? In a misguided attempt to protect you, your ego becomes very defensive, and it will do everything it can to prevent you from registering critical information unless it's offered in exactly the correct way.

Whatever the ego says, denies, or argues against, the truth doesn't have to wound you. It's all a question of priorities. If you continue to buy into the belief that you must maintain the image that you present to others, then that will be your priority, and anything that appears to put a chink in your self-image will seem hostile to you. You'll resist it. Even though everyone sees through your self-image (and if you haven't realized that yet, the exercises in this chapter should remove the scales from your eyes), you'll fight hard to preserve it.

Another option is to say to yourself, "I've had enough of the way I've been living my life, and I want to make a real change. If that means welcoming criticism, swallowing a bitter pill, and growing from it, then that is what I must do, because radical transformation is what I truly want."

ASSIGNMENT

You've built up ways of acting and using defense mechanisms that were developed in childhood. These behaviors give an impression of you to others, but they may be outdated and are probably not working so well anymore. The manner in which people handle stress and anxiety starts taking form when they have very little control—as children. Unfortunately, old habits die hard, and even when choices appear and doors open, you may continue to use these antiquated and inadequate mechanisms. Think back and answer the following questions with as much detail as you can muster:

- How did you react as a child in an attempt to shield yourself from discomfort? Can you think of several incidents?

- How did that defensive pattern develop as you became an adolescent? Was it successful?

- Are you still using the same reaction as an adult, and how is it working?

- What do you need to update?

Keep what you've heard in mind, and observe yourself moving around the world and interacting with others. Be the experimenter. Whereas you have spent the first part of this book documenting, now you are going to watch yourself and see what your knee-jerk reactions are.

Does what you observe remind you of some-one? You might be appalled ("I've turned into my mother!"), or go to the other extreme: "Wow, I wanted to be independent, now I've overachieved it and have become so standoffish that everything about me says, 'I don't need anybody.'" This is a topic to think about long-term. Most of the time you might do things and make big decisions—even as an adult—in an attempt to please your parents, annoy them, or prove your independence. None of these approaches is an exercise of free will. Your parents might not even be alive anymore or care. It's the par-ent you have internalized who is calling the shots.

Just like asking people around you for feedback for this chapter, this assignment is an ongoing one that requires practice. Set a goal to become your own observer: watch yourself (your internal reactions) and note how every action of yours creates a reaction in the world around you. Allow this loop of constant information to help you make better choices, be a better human being, and ultimately feel powerful and present. It's heavy stuff, isn't it?

Giving Is as Hard as Receiving

Most people find it as hard to give constructive criticism as to receive it. If you're the type who wants to shoot the messenger, then you'll be nervous when the shoe is on the other foot and you might be the one to get whacked. Practice giving feedback to others; it will make your relationships more genuine, because honesty is an aspect of authenticity. This will also help you to receive feedback with greater openness, because you'll increasingly view this information for what it truly is: a way in which people who care about each other help each other.

One of the reasons feedback is difficult for you to hear is that you've been raised in a culture of judgment and blame, and being judged and blamed never feels good; however, that's not what you're learning to do here. Your goal should be to provide feedback solely for the purpose of benefiting the other person—and to be forgiving if he or she is not able to accept the feedback at the moment you offer it.

Feedback 101: Here are two basic but silly circumstances in which I tend to give feedback because, well, I'd want to know, wouldn't you?

- Weak handshakes are a pet peeve of mine. When given the dead-fish grip, I'll say, "Oh, no, no, we have to do that over again." I teach people what feels like a meek, uncommitted greeting versus a firm handshake that conveys confidence and warmth.

- Your friend has a piece of lettuce stuck between her teeth. Can you point it out nonchalantly? You both understand that the momentary awkwardness that this causes is compensated many times over by the long-term embarrassment it saves her when she finally notices it hours later.

ASSIGNMENT

Think of five friends you esteem but who each have a maddening habit or trait that no one has ever pointed out to them. Now pretend that they have written to you asking for feedback about their way of presenting themselves to the world. Write five letters, observing how you couch criticism. How would you want the same things said to you?

People tell themselves real friends love them with their faults, unconditionally, for who they are. This is a myth. You can always change for the better. Whether it's an annoying habit, a question of hygiene or etiquette, or a deep-seated intergenerational personality flaw, grab it by the horns and stare it down. There's a new sheriff in town who wants accountability!

A Final Task

Most of the people you asked for feedback didn't really want to give it. It must have been uncomfortable for them. They thought that they'd have to defend themselves later or that it might lead to an argument. So let them off the hook. Answer with e-mails thanking them for giving the feedback. Let them know that you're grateful to have received it and that it is helping you tremendously. Give them the reassurance that you did, in fact, want the kind of information they gave and that you truly appreciate it (say this even to people who were out in left field).

Q and A

Q. How do I become my own observer?

A. As a psychologist, I ask people to watch their reactions: to notice patterns, and, almost as a third person, be the experimenter in noting how they feel or react in different situations. Bringing this information back to the therapy session empowers the patient and also moves the therapy along with true and recent examples. The idea of observing, in which the mind and the brain are separate and the mind interprets the signals the body produces, was written about extensively by the French philosopher René Descartes. Buddhism talks about "mindfulness," a state in which the mind watches itself and lets thoughts come and go and in which one tries not to let the mind wander while one is meditating. Buddhism also states that a person has a calm and stable mind if external surroundings or conditions cause only a limited disturbance. This should definitely be a long-term therapy goal for everyone.

Q. It's hard to be grateful for criticism, even if it is constructive. Do you have any advice?

A. One patient of mine felt better when he came up with his own metaphor: "It's as if a contractor friend of mine comes to my house and finds some termites and a possible fracture. I can't be angry at him; I have to be grateful that he found it before it became a huge problem, right?"

Q. What do you mean by an "internalized" parent?

A. When you are young, you take in the things your parents say; you absorb indiscriminately both the verbal and the nonverbal. You end up with a tape—okay, a CD—of opinions that might actually not be yours at all. They were recorded by your young little brain, and now you assume it all to be true, or you spew out the "party line" without realizing that it isn't really yours. If you don't like what you have internalized, you can choose to test it out in reality to see if it really should be part of your repertoire at all and excise it if you decide that it shouldn't.

DAY SIX

Intermission: Breakdown or Breakthrough?

After today, you'll be halfway through this program. You will be right at the midpoint—50 percent. Has the thought snuck into your head that maybe just getting to this point is good enough? Maybe you've become a little slack, let yourself be interrupted by the phone, glossed over some topics when you know you should dig harder, or convinced yourself that you don't have to write a certain thought down because you'll remember it later. If this is the case, it's time for a pep talk: rev yourself up and refocus.

This is, in fact, the perfect time to discuss exactly how to reinforce your commitment to be a better person, to keep growing and finding the inspiration to continue pushing yourself to be a better version of you. You've come this far in the program because you're sincere about wanting to change. Remind yourself by thinking about days 1 and 2. Remember that accepting this challenge was your decision. Recall the moment you picked up this book. What resounded with you? What made you decide to try it? That was an important step toward change. You probably said to yourself, "This time I mean it. It's going to be different from now on." Get back in touch with that sincerity.

I'm not going to call you names, throw up my hands, or try to incite you by enumerating the people who depend on you, who look up to you, and so forth. What I will do is point out that you have six and a half hours of this superintensive cram course left; that's equivalent to three and a quarter movies (if you count the previews) or the amount of bad TV you'd watch in two and a half days. It's peanuts, really. Do it for yourself.

Go, Me!

Part of what is easy about slacking off in taking care of yourself (physically and emotionally) is that you are the only one who knows. You are also an expert at coming up with reasons for not doing more cardio exercise, drinking more water, and eating more vegetables. After all, chocolate comes from a bean, so it counts as a vegetable, doesn't it? Beer is made from hops, and that's a plant, isn't it?

The flip side is that you seldom acknowledge what you have achieved. What's missing from your life in this respect is positive feedback and good old-fashioned praise. Praise—real, meaningful praise—is something that people don't receive or give nearly enough. They secure the deal, pass the exam, get the pay raise, clean out the garage, or work through the 172 messages in their e-mail account, usually without so much as a pat on the back or a thank you. Perhaps they pause for a moment and feel a brief sense of satisfaction. Soon enough, however, they've got their sights on the next deal, exam, or pay raise. Tomorrow they'll rearrange the stuff in the basement, and the day after that they'll tackle another forty-five e-mails.

Maybe somewhere along the way, your parents drilled into you the fact that you shouldn't toot your own horn, adding, "What you did was good, but you can always do better." You have friends who remind you of your positive characteristics, and every once in a while a boss or a client will throw you a bone of a compliment. There is a big difference, however, between people who can be proud of themselves, give themselves a high-five, and recognize a job well done and those who barely give achievement a thought. For the latter, a victory is checked off a list and they move on, focusing on the next thing that has to be done. Life for them becomes a never-ending "to-do" list. They rarely have a sense of completion; maybe they have come to believe that they don't even need praise. Praise is for kids!

In order to really hear praise, to take it in and have it nourish you, you have to be in the present. You've heard about the value of being in the present, of living in the here and now, of enjoying the moment. It sounds great, but how exactly do you do it? You know all the great clichés—give your soul chicken soup, stop and smell the roses—but no one ever bothers to tell you exactly *how* it's done (other than eating that soup and sniffing those flowers). These are nice ideas, but the instruction manual could use some improvement.

You pause because you are trying to be in the moment, enjoy your success for a few seconds, or bask in a moment

of personal satisfaction or happiness. Then you sheepishly
wonder if anyone is looking, and you dive back into your
to-do list. That kind of rush leaves you very unsatisfied.
Maybe one of the reasons the day flies by so quickly is that
you are running around trying to get things done, believing that you'll enjoy life's sweet rewards later. You think
you'll enjoy them on the weekend, but then there are a
million things to do on the weekend. You'll enjoy them
during your vacation, you say, when the kids leave home,
or when you retire—later, always later.

The ability to celebrate small victories wanes from the
time we are children. Life goes by so quickly, daily activities seem so routine, and many people find themselves
bored or unhappy in the moment because no one is both-
ering to post an adult version of their spelling test with the
big A on the refrigerator. You need to put it up yourself.

It doesn't have to be a major coup to deserve recognition. It can be anything from the mundane to the unusual,
an accomplishment from the workplace or from your
garage. You got something done that you were dreading,
you pushed yourself when just "good enough" would have
been okay, or you were able to be kind and understanding when you normally would have been impatient. Pat
yourself on the back. (Instructions: Swing your arm across
your chest diagonally, let your palm fall over to your back,
and hold your elbow with the other arm. Now, flap your
hand several times and make an audible patting sound on
the back of your shoulder.) Then say: "Good job [insert
your own name here]; very nice, very nice."

Pause for a moment and give yourself some support,
kudos, credit, and positive reinforcement—whatever you
call it. Take a deep breath, puff up your chest, and move
the corners of your mouth up toward your ears. Stretch
both arms out and clap your hands over your head. You

just gave yourself a high-five. Do this more often. It's good for you.

When you have finished patting yourself on the back and clapping your hands over your head, start a "got done" list. Typically, you just cross off whatever you completed on your to-do list, thus focusing only on the things you didn't get done. Get into the habit of noting what you *have* done and acknowledging your accomplishments. Give yourself a reward. It can be something simple, like permission to take a nap without feeling guilty about the million other things you have to do. Buy yourself a celebratory round, or just sit down in your favorite armchair and allow yourself to do nothing for fifteen minutes. Find something that signals to your body that even though life is complicated, you are doing a really good job. You'll be amazed by how much more fulfilled you'll feel.

Do therapists praise? It sounds like a stupid question, but you never see TV or movie therapists clap their hands and exclaim, "Good job!" In real therapy it might be a smile and a nod, or it might be a more motherly reaction or even a hug, but, yes, therapists do praise. This means that while you are acting as your own therapist, you have to give yourself recognition for a job well done.

All right, enough dawdling—let's get back to work.

The Breakdown before the Breakthrough

"Are you fed up enough?" your therapist asks. "Aren't you sick and tired of being sick and tired? Aren't you?" Actually, few therapists would ask that—at least in that way—but getting fed up with your current situation really is a requirement for change. However, if only part of you wants to change, if you aren't thoroughly and completely tired of how things are, you'll sabotage your own efforts.

You'll set unreasonable goals and thereby set yourself up for failure, and failing will convince you that you shouldn't have tried in the first place.

The habit of living in a routine—an uncomfortable one, maybe, but a safe one—has become ingrained. The idea of breaking out of a routine is very hard. Whatever you've been doing—whether it's quashing your creative needs, ignoring a pain in your body, or paying no heed to the emptiness in your heart—it's something you've done hundreds, even thousands, of times. Rocking the boat isn't easy, especially if it's your boat and you're still in it.

Your ambivalence—not liking the *here* but afraid of going *there*—will freeze you in place. (We'll talk more about inertia and momentum soon.) You'll take one step forward and stumble back two, then one forward and one back, only to find yourself still stuck at the starting gate. When a therapist sees patients struggling like this—trying so hard, becoming frustrated by their efforts, trying again, getting angry at people around them, and becoming exasperated with themselves—the therapist knows that it's time to start figuring out what the secondary, and most likely unconscious, benefits of keeping the status quo are.

I know that leaving familiar circumstances and altering beliefs can be difficult. Down deep you may hear a little voice saying, "What happens if I regret the changes I've made and can't go back?" or "Isn't asking for more a way of being greedy? Won't I be punished for it?" Don't let these thoughts hold you back; listen to the part of you that says it is frustrated and wants change. It's the voice that says, after you have spent half an hour looking for a receipt, that this is the last straw: now you will take the time to organize your files. You trip hard over the same box in the garage so often that you finally pick it up and throw it away. Do you know that feeling? It's time to unclutter, move, file, or discard the stumbling blocks in your emotional life.

One of the most important psychological theories of change states that if you are not uncomfortable, you won't move. Therefore, if you are waffling, or if in the past have sabotaged your own efforts to gauge what's going on, your therapist might ask the following questions:

- Is your goal in therapy to be happy with what you have?
- Do you want to change only because you think you *should* change?
- Can you pinpoint where the unhappiness with your current state comes from?
- Are you ambivalent about change?
- Should we look for a third possibility for change that you haven't considered?

When asking yourself these questions, be brutally honest with what your goals are. If *change* is your goal, you need to look yourself in the eye and ask, "Are you sure?" If you have the tiniest hesitation, anything short of a wholehearted "Absolutely," and you are not completely committed to the idea that you can sustain the effort at 100 percent, then there is a preliminary step you have to take in order to determine why not.

This minor but vital move is one that many people fail to make. It is this part of the instructions that is key. You've heard your friends and people on TV proclaim, "I'm sick of being fat, lonely, financially unstable, or unhappily married." So why don't they do something about it? They have to take this one small step to make sure that nothing is holding them back.

Whenever you want to make a change, you have to take this step to see what could get in your way. You might not even be aware of some of the obstacles. You have to literally scan your emotional and historical landscape in order to see what land mines lie in your path. Are any of the following familiar?

- I'm afraid, plain and simple, and the fear is trumping my discomfort.
- I can always hear my mother's voice saying that wanting more is greedy.
- I keep thinking I'll somehow get punished for asking for more.
- I hate to admit it, but despite the fact that I hate my life the way it is, there are subtle perks that I get from the situation.
- I'm lazy. I know that getting there and staying there will be harder than just staying here.
- My spouse, friend, or family says it's the right thing to do, but *I'm* not sure I want to do it.
- Failing is painful. I'd rather stay still.
- If I stay here, I can wallow in self-pity, and frankly, that doesn't feel so bad sometimes.
- It's such a daunting move; I can't even figure out where to start.
- Society tells me that this is what I should want, but deep down inside, I don't know if I care.

Your logical brain weighs the situation and wants to go, go, go. Then the part of your brain that has created the neurological pathways that make life easy, safe, tolerable, and habitual begins to resist (more on this soon). Added to this scenario are the irrational ideas that either slow you down or are so grandiose they set you up to fail. If you haven't disarmed these thoughts, they'll shoot you down in the most insidious ways.

ASSIGNMENT

I want to shore up your chances of completing this program successfully. I don't have the luxury of saying, "Oh, maybe in another month; we'll move this along slowly." You and I have eight more days together. This chapter is therefore about pinpointing where you might trip yourself up so that we can troubleshoot. Unlike traditional therapy, in which the therapist can eventually detect if you're fooling or belittling yourself, in self-therapy you have the ability to convince yourself of anything and not even know you're doing it—and that's dangerous.

Start by writing down ten lies or exaggerations that you tell (or have told) about yourself. I'll give you a hand with some examples. The lie: "I could be further along in life, but I have a short attention span." The truth: When it's something you don't like, it's hard to keep at it. It's a question of a lack of motivation or a low frustration tolerance. We all prefer to do what we do well and easily. The lie: "I have a strong personality that not everyone can handle; I have high energy and an impulsive nature." The truth: So does every four-year-old out there. It's time to work on this one. The lie: "I'm not detail oriented, I'm a big-picture kind of person." The truth: You aren't paying attention. See the first example.

If you're feeling anxious or bored in this process, you've rattled your unconscious, opened Pandora's box or that can of worms inside yourself, and shaken things up. Maybe your psyche is used to getting this far, however; you've done it a bunch of times, so you don't feel any anxiety. In fact, you are looking forward to today's exercise—bring it on. If this is the case, this time you should aim to dig deeper, to pry things open and really get down and dirty. Give yourself a high-five for getting through the first assignment and tackle the next one.

ASSIGNMENT

As I said earlier, intellectually wanting to make a change doesn't mean that you're ready to actually do so. It only means that your logical brain has come to the realization that it would be good for you to make a move. The next step, then, is figuring out what has kept you waffling (or taking the two steps back), which means determining what you'd miss if you changed your current situation, even if it is minuscule. This assignment requires some real heart-wrenching self-examination. You are about to take a long look at the secondary gains I mentioned earlier. To help you along, I'll share with you some of the benefits my patients have derived from uncomfortable situations:

- I get attention from people who are concerned about my condition, so if I fix the condition, I won't get the attention. I hate to say it, but the pity and the hugs feel good. Sometimes I know my situation isn't even that bad, and I exaggerate it for effect.

- Not moving on in my breakup lets me be angry with my ex. I almost enjoy feeling scorned. Otherwise I'd have to admit that getting over it and dating again are terrifying.

- In order to make some real changes, I'd have to wholeheartedly admit that I don't like where I am in life. The fact that I've put in all this effort to get here and am not happy makes me think that I've wasted my time and made bad decisions. It's easier to pretend that I am okay.

Start writing, and note what happened the last time you tried to change this. What happened? How are you going to ensure that it doesn't happen again?

ASSIGNMENT

The next step is to talk about why your motivation has reached a plateau—if not now, at some other point in your life. Perhaps you're thinking that you know what is wrong with you. At least you're close. Part of you hears things like "At least my life is predictable," "I'm just a whiner," "I'm not smart, strong, or brave enough," "I actually like myself the way I am," or "I am what I am." Maybe a big part of you thinks that in some way you deserve this "punishment," or maybe it is something you have to deal with and learn to ignore. Perhaps you'll get used to it, or perhaps you really are asking for too much.

The bottom line is that somewhere, somehow, you've decided that your understanding is good enough as it is, that changing in order to become better or more comfortable is asking too much. Recognize that these are your defenses kicking in, that this is exactly when you have to commit yourself to a course of action and keep moving forward. Keep telling yourself that you are worth the effort and the time.

Now I'm going to ask you to be more specific. I'll give you a start with the following exercise:

1. Finish this sentence: "Really embracing change is hard because . . ." Some answers could be as follows: "Other people depend on me, and it's selfish of me to rock the boat." "Things will get worse, and I'll be punished for wanting more." "There is something I really enjoy about being a martyr." Whatever your answer is, write it out. Keep in mind that this is not what you know you *should* be thinking, it's whatever thought comes into your head.

2. Determine your locus of control. Psychological theory says that depressed people have an external locus of control: they see life's events happening *to* them. Contented people have an internal locus of control: they experience themselves as empowered and proactive. Happy people perceive bad things as transient rather than ongoing, and they take credit for the good things that happen to them. Depressed people, on the other hand, see bad things as coming at them from the outside and good things as the result of luck. This attitude is not something that you can change overnight. The whole concept of control has to stew in your thoughts for a while. As you experiment, remember that you do have choices, and look deliberately at how you interpret events.

   Now look at your current situation and ask yourself how much of you is waiting for change to be made by outside forces and how much is ready to change whatever you control. This exercise will help you to understand that although you are a product of where you came from, you have the choice not to be that way anymore. A therapist would encourage you to recognize the difference between being a child without choices and being an adult with choices and the will to exercise different options.

3. As you write about change and control, take a situation you've always thought of as being externally controlled, as having a resolution effected by something or someone else. Even if it seems like a complete daydream, don't revert to the script you've had forever. For a few minutes, write about "If I could," "If I knew how," and "If for one day things were different." Examine what you've written. Do all the situations require the help of a superhero to be realized? Are there any ways you could move closer to your goal, even by an inch? Are there any parts of the daydream you could experience, savor for even a minute, just to give yourself incentive? How has considering these things externally solvable kept you waiting and immobile?

I know that it's getting harder at this point, but root for yourself to take on the next assignment.

ASSIGNMENT

Now I want you to think of every association to change that you can. After having completed the first three assignments, you know that there are reasons you are getting in your own way. Pinpoint them and connect the dots. Write down your responses to the following questions. Go into as much detail as you can. Free-associate freely, wildly, and with gusto!

1. What are all the very possible and the very farfetched reasons you haven't met your psychological and emotional goals in the past?

2. What about the third or fourth option that you know exists but have not, in fact, seriously considered? Is it perhaps the halfway point between two choices, or does it go off in the opposite direction? Why is each choice attractive or not?

3. What fears are keeping you back? What secondary gains are holding you in place?

4. Are you thoroughly and unequivocally sick of being here and totally ready to be there? Can you say it out loud? Does it sound right?

5. Write down your hesitations and doubts. Just because you have them doesn't mean you won't get to where you want to go. Keeping them in line will help you to devise a better plan.

6. Think back on how you dealt with change as a kid. Were you fearless, or were you terrible at coping with transitions? How were you as an adolescent? As a young adult?

You've been digging deep. Are you feeling anxious at this point? You might be experiencing a secondary type of anxiety called *learning anxiety*. It is characterized by the feeling that if people allow themselves to enter a learning or change process and admit to themselves and others that something is wrong or imperfect, they will lose their effectiveness, their self-esteem, and perhaps even their identity.

Human beings need to assume that they are doing their best at all times, and it can be a real loss of face (and faith) to accept and even embrace errors. Adapting poorly or failing to meet one's creative potential often looks more desirable than risking failure and loss of self-esteem in the learning process. Keep going, praise yourself for coming this far, and know that the feelings of anxiety mean that you are doing some real work.

ASSIGNMENT

Let's finish by going back to the beginning. Write about being almost halfway there. Recall the things you have done and give a description of reaching that 50 percent. Regardless of whether the changes were small or big events, what did they look like? What did you do? Do you remember when you have committed yourself to a big project? How did you think about it? Did you immediately start making a list of what had to be done, or did you rest up in order to be able to think clearly about it? If you were at work, did you jump to your computer and start the project, or did you turn off the computer, go home, put things in order there, and have a good night's sleep?

How are you feeling about the steps you've taken so far? Are there exercises you skimmed over, that you are feeling guilty about because you did them too quickly? As long as you have done most of the work wholeheartedly, even battling with yourself to sit still and tell the truth, you've come close to what you might have accomplished with a top-notch Park Avenue therapist. Don't say, "Aw, shucks, it was no big deal." Take the compliment. Absorb and relish the praise.

Q and A

Q. How am I supposed to learn to be in the moment?

A. Try to stop yourself from thinking about the past or the future for a few minutes. It's harder than you think. The most common way is to focus on your breathing. If you are concentrating on your inhalations and exhalations and not letting your mind wander, then you are training yourself to be in the moment more, to be more present. The funny thing is that if you try it, you'll see that it is so much harder than you ever thought. You'll focus on the air coming into your lungs, feel it coming out your nostrils, then find yourself wondering what is for dinner, realize that you have an itch on your foot, and wonder what that noise outside is. You'll try again and get to the third or fourth breath. It takes a lot of mental discipline. You'll find that worrying, planning, complaining, and looking forward to upcoming events are all easier—but none of those activities is in the moment.

The idea from the last chapter of becoming more mindful is related. Your thoughts are not the essence of who you are. Underneath all the chatter in your head you'll find a peacefully quiet place that is in the moment—it's just that you have no practice getting there and staying there, and your complicated life doesn't allow you the time to work at it. It's there, however, that you can ask yourself important questions and get real clear answers. In addition, you'll feel more stable. Being able to put yourself in a safe trancelike state of calmness while concentrating on your breathing will teach you not to be thrown around by events and information in your life. You'll feel strong because despite what is on the news and what is chaotic in your life, you'll know how to calm yourself. It's complicated stuff, so take a meditation class, a breathing class, or a yoga class, or buy a breathing instruction DVD from a company like Sounds True to get you on your way.

DAY SEVEN

Look Back, Then Look Forward

This book is your practical, cut-to-the-chase guide on how to solve your emotional problems, so let's cut to the chase. Today you have to motivate yourself, focus, and get through this lecture and assignment as if you were digging a tunnel to break out of Alcatraz—no whining, sighing, or feeling sorry for yourself. When you have any of those feelings, call yourself on it, whether by telling yourself not to be a "spineless jerk" (no, that's not my opinion of you—it's just an example) or choosing more positive words like "You can do this! You are worth it! Yes—go, baby go—yes!"

First, go back and skim your writings of the last week. Using a highlighter, a red pen, or the boldface button on your computer, mark the attitudes, reactions, behaviors, patterns, or excuses that stand out. By "stand out," I mean that they are repeated verbatim, they show up in different versions, or you see one of them just once but get a gut feeling that this is important.

Don't ignore that feeling; trust your instincts. Don't censor yourself or start editing. Be the therapist. Sit in another seat from your usual one and be the one who is listening and watching for slips of the tongue, stutters, telling body language, or tiny flinches in the writing that might be covering a huge volcano of information. You can circle, underline, highlight, or boldface lots of things. Don't be afraid of "ruining" the page. Don't be neat, don't be picky. Do this fast, page after page, and get into a rhythm. If something stands out as being repetitious, ironic, humorous, or infantile—anything that makes you bristle, feel ashamed, or even amused—mark it and move on to the next page.

Don't fall into the trap of being distracted from the real job by judging your writing. Remember what I said about not censoring yourself or starting to edit. Imagine that these words were written by someone else—a third person—and keep your inner literary critic out of the process. Be objective and take a practical approach, just as you would if you were looking for specific washing instructions on a sweater's tag, the expiration date on a container of milk, a customer service number, or the required dose for some cold medicine.

ASSIGNMENT

Stay firmly in a practical and analytical frame of mind. After marking up your writing, answer these questions as if you were examining the behavior of a third person:

1. What is this person's goal in therapy?

2. What does this person need to do to be happy?

3. What is holding this person back?

4. How can the obstacles that are keeping this person from changing be overcome?

5. What answers or solutions does this person have right in front of his or her face but doesn't see?

Now breathe deeply and switch mental channels.

ASSIGNMENT

Read the following paragraph out loud:

> When I first started reading, writing, and doing this work, I wasn't quite sure where it was going to take me. Now it's clearer; my goals seem easier to articulate. Maybe I understand how complex this project is or how much power I have to start moving. Now I see more clearly where I stand. I definitely feel more grounded and believe that I can work and change. I know I have the answers; I just have to find the right questions to bring them out.

Reassure yourself as your therapist would: "Sure, maybe I'm a little anxious, but I am starting to understand that this is the kind of work that involves many steps and a lot of going back and forth. I can do it. It's a process."

Maybe "a little anxious" doesn't describe your present state. Change it, maybe, to "restless and impatient" or even "really terrified." These are your writings—you are the author. Remind yourself that this is a process that winds and stalls or leaps forward unexpectedly. You are standing at the very center of it. While you go through your day, your writings are stirring things up inside and doing therapy work even when you aren't thinking about it.

Your Power Statement

You've now reached a turning point in the process. By pouring your uncensored thoughts into your journal, you have made the "invisible you" visible. You've given yourself the opportunity to see more clearly the thoughts, beliefs, and assumptions that have been influencing your life and, for the most part, influencing it negatively. Now it's time to start changing direction. This is where a power statement comes in.

Stop sneering; it's not corny. It's like your "coming out on stage" song, the tune you play when you are getting psyched to go out and do something significant. Think of a movie line or a motto that inspires you no matter how many times you hear it. It's time to write yours.

A power statement can have a business feel to it. Patients shy away from such a concept because it sounds mechanical. It sounds too serious or contrived for abstract feelings and reactions, hopes and hurts. Some patients prefer the term *mantra*, which is more like a prayer or an affirmation. Perhaps you like the sound of a "little engine that could" type of sentence that is comforting and that focuses, inspires, or calms you when you need it.

Call it whatever you want. Maybe you are comfortable with the idea of a personal or power statement, or maybe in your work you use contracts, so you can relate to that concept. Whatever you call it, it's like a contract plus a prayer with a sprinkling of favorite inspirational song lyrics. It is a declaration of what you intend to experience and achieve from this point forward in your life; therefore, you must take the time to elaborate it, write it down, and memorize it. Put it to music. Then post your power statement where you can see it every morning to remind yourself of your mission: to understand, to see your choices, to change your life in however big or small a way is necessary.

You definitely need to do this. It's not a big deal. If you are bristling and don't really want to do it, however, confront that feeling in yourself. Why are you being a baby or a scaredy-cat? Why are you suddenly thinking that there's something very important you need to do in another room?

Just pretend it's a rough draft. No one will see it. It's not going to be framed or read out loud in front of groups of people. It's your mission statement, and you need it; you deserve it. (If I asked you to "roast," or make fun of, yourself, you'd most likely have no problem doing so. You'd poke fun at every fault, wrinkle, bad joke, misstep, or stupid idea you ever had. Why, then, is saying good things so much harder? Think about it.)

Let's take it step by step; at the end we'll pull it all together.

1. Start with a sentence that summarizes who you are deep inside or your life goal. It can be original or inspired by a song, a poem, or a movie: "Everything's gonna be all right," or "So often it happens that we live our life in chains, and we never even know we

have the key. I'm going to find my key." "Nobody puts Baby in a corner." "It's a new dawn, it's a new day, it's a new life, for me, and I'm feeling good."

2. The next line should start with "I'm working hard at . . ." and then you add things you know you are in the process of figuring out, according to the work you've done in the past week.

3. The next line should be "I will be able to . . ." with an additional sentence or two about your goals. Always keep in mind that this is a process, that there will be steps forward and backward.

4. Finish with a statement that recognizes this process. Be both realistic and kind to yourself: "Life is a process and, I am grateful for . . ." You have tons to write here. Don't hold back, and give yourself credit! End up with something like "My soul, my body, and my brain deserve and need care, and I commit to taking care of myself."

I'm really pushing you, aren't I? Sometimes you need a push, albeit a loving one.

Years ago I started using what I called the "forced poetry" technique (I'm sure there's a nicer term, but I didn't know of any back then) when I was working in New York City hospitals with adolescents. They didn't want to be there, had nothing to say, and were generally angry, often very understandably so. They would give me one-word answers, so I made up a technique that required only one word. I told them that they'd be writing lyrics, free verse, and poetry and that I'd start by asking questions.

Me: How are you today?

Patient: Mad.

Me: If your anger were a color, what would it be?

Patient: This is stupid.

Me: Okay, but just tell me a color. It's no big deal.

Patient: Red. No, black. Yeah, black.

Me: How about an animal?

Patient: Easy. Panther.

Me: What kind?

Patient: What do you mean, what kind? You know, a long one, with big teeth.

Me: Prowling or running?

Patient: No, you know. Like stalking. Yeah. Stalking.

Me: How does it make you feel to see him?

Patient: Like up close? Scared s—tless, wouldn't you be? What are you typing? Can I see that? I said "s—tless." You didn't write that. Oh, I guess you shouldn't; okay. Can you print that?

I would then type their words into sentences that I had preformatted. Most liked the idea of a personal secretary and would sit up, feeling very comfortable dictating. Once I was finished, I would print it out, stand up, clear my throat, then add a title, with the patient's name as the author, and read it out loud as dramatically as possible.

Teens who were practically mute started coming to therapy enthusiastically; they would shush me and start to rattle off descriptions of feelings, leaving after their session with pages and pages, booklets of poems. One patient won a poetry contest in his school. He was exuberant, recalling his teachers' surprised faces when he was announced the winner: "Yeah, me? Believe it? Uh-huh, that's right!"

This is the move I am encouraging, therefore, when I say that you should sit down and write your power statement. Once you feel the poet in you start to stir, let him or her out!

You can amend your power statement once a year or every month. This minimizes chasing-your-tail behavior. It's like writing your New Year's resolutions but updating them throughout the whole year. Updating your statement or contract is something you should do to exercise your brain and to keep yourself focused and constantly refreshing yourself, as you would on a computer.

ASSIGNMENT

Write your power statement, using the outline above or whatever works for you. It's very important that what you write is in your own words, not word-for-word repetitions of the "deep thoughts" of Jack Handey, perky pointers from your company's motivational sales pitches, or phrases with Dr. Phil's southern homespun inflections. Pick your own voice. I can hear you saying, "What does that mean, Doc? Come on, now, in English."

When I say "pick your own voice," I mean that you should think about exactly what you sound like when you talk to yourself and say things such as "It's not that bad" or "It will get better" and really believe it. I want you to find a levelheaded tone that sympathizes but is rational, too. Contrast it to the one that is your crybaby ("I'm going to die if I stay at this job one minute longer!") or your drill sergeant ("Get off your butt, right now, grunt!"). Pick the one that has the tone of "It's going to sting for a minute, but we'll

put a bandage on it and you'll heal in no time" or
"Come on; it's heavy, but if you pick it up from that
side, we can move it up the stairs together."

ASSIGNMENT

Sit for a minute and think about the voice with which
you talk to yourself. Are there several voices in your
head, each for a different occasion? We've already
talked about acknowledging the parental voice that
can try to run—and at times, ruin—your life. Now
make a list of all the types of voices that you hear at
various times.

Not all of them will be bad voices. You might have
had a kind and wise uncle or grandmother whose
words you still remember. How about the voice that
is your intuition, that tells you to check something
one more time or to be wary of a certain circumstance
because it just doesn't sound quite right? Think of
different situations you've been in, and make a list
of five voices that pop into your head and influence
your behavior.

To get you started, I'll list the most common:
mother, father, boss (or other authority figure), sib-
ling, best friend. Notice the tone, the pitch, and the
volume of each voice. Write down everything that
occurs to you about that voice, and if you are really
on a roll, write about a specific occasion when you
did or didn't pay attention to it and what the consequences were.

ASSIGNMENT

You've finished the first draft of your power state-ment. Are you ready to move on to the next, more advanced version? Start each sentence with "I will . . ." and then write down the specifics. Let me give you an example. If you state, "I will lead a healthy life," you have to follow that up with details: "I will eat more thoughtfully, I will plan my meals, and I will exercise twenty minutes every day."

Your power statement should address the key issues you have already identified. Use the following as guides:

- I will not be a victim of circumstances. I know that I have choices and that there are alterna-tives. I will make my decisions only after exam-ining them and deciding which are best for me and my goals.

- I will be my own person. I will not live with old myths or let others define me. I will praise myself when I need praise, I will call myself on the need to refocus.

- I will move ahead with my career. I will take the extra course I need, attend workshops that add to my knowledge of the field, and revise my résumé.

Make sure you stay positive. Of course you want to mention how lousy, confused, and freaked out you feel, but that is not what your statement is supposed to do. Write that in your journal. Avoid sentences such as the following:

My life has passed me by, but . . .

I feel mediocre.

I am fat because I don't have willpower.

I haven't forgiven. I am still angry about . . .

I am stupid for letting this drag me down.

Turn these statements around and rephrase them in the positive, even if it sounds like a stretch.

Why It Works

When you elaborate a power statement, you are taking a step that helps you to learn to take care of yourself—yes, *learn*. You will be repeating a construct that you have to absorb in different modalities: by thinking of it, writing it, saying it, repeating it, and subscribing to it. It sounds a lot like learning a topic in school, doesn't it?

In therapy sessions, your therapist would note how you learn—the subtle ways and modes that you employ to take in information. This is something that has been happening throughout this series of sessions, from the very first one. In what manner do you absorb information the best? You pay attention to this yourself in your daily life when you pick a time to tell your spouse something important. You know there are specific times that people don't seem to process information well and other times that they do. Your therapist would notice words that serve as triggers for you and would discern how you react to different tones of voice and respond to tactics that help you to remember.

Standard IQ tests recognize the traditional intellectual style of learning. However, other types of intelligence, like emotional IQ or social IQ, have become better known recently. In therapy—and in reading this book—you might find things that don't make sense, that you don't understand because they aren't in the right modality for your brain. Don't give up; keep working at it, searching for what works for you. Realize that children with learning disabilities can learn just as quickly if their instructors recognize their style of learning and utilize their strengths rather than sticking to rigid ways of teaching.

Sophisticated television shows and books for children take this into account: they take a topic and write about it, sing about it, and make a dance about it. Whether they use Schoolhouse Rock or a friendly, fuzzy puppet, they operate on the assumption that being taught and reminded of information in different modalities is the best way to process and retain data.

Power statements use the same logic. You've read and written about different topics. We've discussed and expanded on various themes. I've asked you to fantasize and make wish lists; I've told you to be very practical. The consistency and repetition of a power statement will nudge you along even further: you will accept the new paradigm of change on your own.

Reading It Out Loud

Read your power statement out loud ten times—not five, not eight, but ten. Make little marks to keep count. Keep at it until you can recite it flawlessly by heart. This is vital, because those other voices, the ones that have been running and ruining your life, are deeply rooted inside you. You need to be able to conjure up your mantra quickly and convincingly in retaliation.

Your power statement specifies what you want out of life and should detail how you are going to get it. You might not get it all soon, and you might change your mind later, but for now you have your eyes on the prize as you see it today. You've narrowed it down further and further and said, "That one, that one there, that is what I want."

This is what the power statement does: it makes you focus, gives you confidence, and helps you to choose your goals and spells them out. It takes pining and wishing to a new level. It's a plan—maybe without an exact road map, but it will keep you moving in the right general direction. It's simple, but it's really powerful.

Do you still hear an earlier version of yourself, or maybe someone else—a friend or a family member—in the corner of your mind, muttering, "This is silly"? Tell that voice to shut up. Tell it that you are tired of things the way they are and that you chose to ignore it—period. You already know how to do this: you tell your kids to hush when they are whining; you walk away from your mother when she's complaining about things she can't control; you tune out the TV when you are on the phone.

Choose a spot where you will recite your power statement every morning. For the next seven days, your assignment is to do this right after your writing session. If you are disciplined, you can pick a different time: at the door before you set out to face the world, in the office after you take off your jacket and get ready to work with disparate types of people. You can repeat it anytime during the day when you need to be "recalibrated," when you feel the need to focus on your real goals in life, or when you fear that you are slipping back into old thoughts that drag you down.

Say your power statement to yourself as you would
to a child who needs to be comforted, or say it as a
declaration to the world. Find the attitude that works
for you. Do it for the next week, starting today, starting
right now.

Q and A

Q. Where did this idea of a personal, or mission, statement come from?

A. Affirmations of intent are words that are used to
articulate one's mission. In business, it originates from a
management guru by the name of W. Edwards Deming,
who transformed the Japanese automobile industry in
the 1950s with his theory of quality management. Small
Japanese cars were suddenly outselling and outperform-
ing trusty American Buicks and Fords. Deming insisted
that every corporation (or any entity) have a mission
statement and, more important, that every employee
know it.

Q. You mention refreshing your thoughts and compare that to something you'd do on a computer. I'm
not really technologically savvy, so that doesn't resonate
with me. Do you have any other examples?

A. Horses will flutter their lips and snort to "recali-
brate." It's the standing up and stretching that you do
at a meeting to try to stay alert. Think about eating
sorbet between the courses of a meal to clear your
palate; or, if you are into scents, think of how you
would smell coffee beans in between sniffing different
perfumes.

Q. When are the voices in your head a metaphor and when are they serious mental illness?

A. Psychotic hallucinations are very different from the internalized voices of authority figures that you hear running through your head. Auditory hallucinations that are part of psychoses can be anything from mumbles to frightening commands. Antipsychotic medication can quiet these voices, which are the result of brain chemistry gone awry. Internalized voices, however, are ideas repeated to you by your parents that you've taken on as your own.

Internal and External Practical Work: Steps to Get There

Because this is a crash course, in this chapter I'm going to blend together several schools of thought in the field of psychology. We'll take a look at some cognitive behavioral techniques, I'll give you some shortcuts on negative thinking patterns and self-talk, and I'll throw in some rational emotive therapy for good measure. There are dozens of books that deal with each approach, but because I am summarizing them for you, I'll just scratch the surface—you'll have to take it to the next level.

As a therapist, when my patients reach the point that you did on day 7, I consider their goals and carefully study how they encourage or discourage themselves in the process.

In other words, what are the thoughts, or cognitions, that are getting in their way? How do unrealistic expectations contribute to failure? What are the series of cognitions, the self-talk, and the irrational thoughts that are holding them back?

Then I examine the positives: What are their strengths in figuring out how to get to where they want to be? Which productive strategies do they use when they problem-solve? What good habits do they already possess that they need to become more conscious of and, consequently, to reinforce? Finally, what rational and reasonable steps do they need to take to attain their goals?

This chapter and the next are superpractical chapters, cookbook instructions, a clear and straightforward connect-the-dots approach. If something is heavy, why do you insist on dragging it around with you? Put it down. If something is in your way, stop tripping on it repeatedly. Go around it. Albert Ellis, the founder of rational emotive behavior therapy, became more direct, cantankerous, and outspoken in his old age. It was not unlike him to bellow things like "If it's not working, stop it" at volunteers from the audience during his immensely popular Friday lectures in New York City, which ran from the mid-sixties to the end of his life in 2007.

You are the one who has been saying, "Give me feedback, just tell me what to do," right? You are the one who has been protesting that "holding hands and singing folk songs" isn't going to cut it for you. You've always had a sense of what is wrong, but you haven't known how to fix it.

Now is the time to get down to the nuts and bolts. You want a Navy SEALs', Outward Bound school of therapy, a two-semester program in one weekend. Would it be nicer to have *The Sopranos*'s calm, impenetrable Dr. Melfi or

Star Trek's beautiful counselor Troi coaching you three times a week for the next year or two? In real life, you might have to meet with several therapists before you find one who really jibes with your personality. While you are considering this, make good use of your time and keep reading and journaling.

This is not superficial therapy for patients with short attention spans; it's therapy for a supermotivated, grab-life-by the-horns person. It's for the person who says, "Tell me what to do, I want to feel better; enough pussyfooting around. Give me a push into the water; I will swim. I'll do the work. I'm ready. It might not all make sense at the moment, but this is a process and I want to be an active participant. Let's get this party started."

So far you've vented daily, which has sorted out the irritants of daily life from the real pain, and you've homed in on your issues by chipping away at some of them from the outside. If you missed a day, give yourself a break. This program has allowed you to think and to organize your thoughts. You've researched and examined your evolution, and you shouldn't have a "How did I get on this crazy ride?" feeling anymore. The ride might still be shaky, but you know how you got here. You are aware of the fact that you stumbled, walked, or sailed through childhood with good, bad, or mediocre parents, and you've accumulated tons of memories along the way (more than you ever imagined, you've now discovered).

In short, you weren't spawned, you didn't crawl out of the water onto the beach on your own, and you weren't hurled into the world from a cyclone. You've thought about the impression you give people around you, you've examined the thoughts you have about yourself, and you've finally become clearer about where you want to be—and it sure isn't right here, right now. So now we'll take your issues, problems, or goals and study them in detail in order to figure them out, then we'll break them up, pop them into a metaphorical blender, and hit "grate." In this chapter and the next, we'll start putting some psychological theory into practice.

Self-help guru Wayne Dyer has said, "Be miserable. Or motivate yourself. Whatever has to be done, it's always your choice." Changing your thought process and motivating yourself to action (from whining to packing, or from pouting to updating your résumé) is the goal. The key is to stop thinking about why you can't, how it will never work, or why bother trying. You should start to take small reasonable steps in the right direction, even if the final destination is far away.

Do you wish you could just be told an easy answer about how to fix your life? Everyone does. "Why didn't my family therapist of five years just come out and tell me the truth?" you moan. Therapy simply doesn't work that way; the patient has to actually walk the long hard road to find the answers. In fact, if your therapist had told you on day one to "leave him, he'll never change" or "she's crazy, head for the hills," you still would have hung on for a good while.

Even you easily recognize why some of your friends always find themselves in hot water, but do they ever listen to you? More important, do you always tell them? All too often you end up losing a friend who didn't take your advice, anyway. Most people resent the messenger who tells them the hard truths. Well-meaning friends can spell out the reasons for their pain until they are blue in the face.

There is something that has to "click," however, because, in the end, only you know, for example, that your spouse is emotionally abusive and won't change. Only you know that your job won't make you happier next year. Only you know that your boyfriend or girlfriend is out of the relationship and is just hanging around because he or she feels sorry for you. Even when you do classic face-to-face therapy, when you finally come to these conclusions, you usually sigh and say, "I knew it; somewhere deep inside, I knew."

Getting you to do this on your own is our next challenge.

ASSIGNMENT

Start with "I want to succeed, but . . ." and finish the sentence with the following phrases:

- What keeps getting in my way is . . .
- What I can't seem to do is . . .
- What keeps bringing me back to step one is . . .
- When things start going wrong, the negative self-talk I hear says . . .
- The person who sabotages my efforts is . . .
- The cycle that is hard to break has to do with . . .
- The main thing I fear that holds me back is . . .

Now, in a completely unemotional, objective way, make a list of the possible resolutions to these seven situations. What pattern can you see? These feelings and situations will come up in your life repeatedly, so look at them as something you have to solve *now*, because they aren't going away on their own.

ASSIGNMENT

Act as if you have made a simple decision to feel different. It's as if an actor were about to go out on stage with a script in his hand, and the director came over and scratched out the cue on the script that says "Character seems worried, hesitant; his past experience is creating fear; he frowns," and replaced it with "Character seems concerned, takes a deep breath, squares his shoulders and grins, knowing he's going to give it his best shot, it's the best he can do."

Play with this idea during the day. If a vending machine eats your change, and you want to slam it and curse at it, stop and try a different reaction. Shrug and think to yourself, "Seventy-five cents, phooey. I hope the next person gets two of what he or she wants. I really shouldn't be eating barbecue-flavored, trans fat–laden cheese curls, anyway." If you are usually a shrug-it-off kind of person, try the opposite. This particular exercise isn't about being more easygoing, it's about learning that you can *decide* to react in different ways.

For this assignment, describe three situations in which you change from reacting in an emotional, unthinking way to a determined, thoughtful way. Think of your mind as being separate from your thoughts. Your thoughts are something you can decide to have one way or another. Actually *decide* what reaction to have. Don't skimp on this one; go into detail.

ASSIGNMENT

Do you ever find yourself having irrational thoughts? "Nah," you say, "I'm a pretty sane person." You'd be surprised how most people harbor at least one idea that is out in left field. How about a belief that defies logic or lacks a rational explanation? It might be that Prince(ss) Charming exists and will show up at your door one day; that you simply haven't *found* the right diet or product to make you lose weight; that if you just try harder, your parents will be happier; that you really don't mind feeling stuck, because frustration is just part of what happens when you grow up.

List your irrational beliefs: the ones that feel dicey, that slow you down and make you doubt; the ones you wish you didn't believe in, but you just can't help it. Expose the illogical, unreasonable, pain-in-the-neck beliefs that keep tripping you up and dragging you back. Remember that no one else will see this; don't worry if you find yourself blushing at some beliefs that are almost superstitions. Write them down!

Inflated worst-case scenarios can get in the way of your getting where you want to go. One reason you don't walk around the boulder of a problem or try to move it is that you overestimate how momentous the consequences of change will be. Some patients utter statements that border on the ridiculous: "If I were to quit, the company would really suffer"; "If I left her, it would kill my mother-in-law"; "If I moved out of state to take that job, I would never have friends"; "If I broke up with him, he would never love again." Other patients step so far ahead that they manage to get in their own way. One patient clung to the idea that losing weight would leave her saddled with yards and yards of extra skin, and then what would she do?

In this chapter, therefore, put aside all the reasons you can't make a change in your life. Go through the motions—the point here is to do the exercise. This could end up being like a fire drill for you, but when you do decide to get up and go for real, you'll have a better result. Neuropsychology explains how rehearsing, even in your head, gives you better results than doing something hastily and unprepared. This is just plain old-fashioned visualizing, but with a hard-core practical element that puts it in a different category.

People practice for future events all the time. They rehearse conversations they are going to have, try on outfits they are going to wear for a special occasion, train for sports in which they are going to compete, prepare speeches or presentations they are going to give, and even rehearse jokes they are going to tell. Yet for some reason they do not prepare for emotional situations. You are now using daily problem-solving techniques (all the exercises and sorting out you did in days 1 through 7) to practice fixing your emotional problems. That is the work you need to do to move the boulder that is your problem; once you do, you will realize that it was much lighter than you ever thought.

ASSIGNMENT

Think of your issues and list them in one column. In a second column, write the simple, obvious solution to each one. I know that this is not always realistic.

Simple solutions are not always possible, but just try the best you can and avoid mental contortions. We are starting out extremely basic, so don't become exasperated. Here are some examples to help you along.

Problem	Solution
I hate myself because I'm fat.	Lose weight.
I'm lonely.	Join clubs.
I can't get a date.	Subscribe to a dating service.
I have low self-esteem.	Stop putting yourself down.
I'm not passionate about anything.	Take up hobbies you enjoyed as a child or adolescent.

Now take a look at your two columns. Pick one item, any one, and commit to doing it. I can hear you groan, "But Dr. Belisa, it's not that simple!" I am not saying it is. This is an exercise. Pick up the metaphorical dumbbell (that is, your pen) and give me twelve more reps.

People tell themselves that change is a long, laborious process, achievable only after a decade of therapy, if even then. There is one thing you can be sure of: if you subscribe to that theory, you'll be right. Your beliefs are self-fulfilling prophecies. Therefore, why not believe that you can take charge of your psychological life and problem-solve, just as you would with practical matters?

When it's raining, you don't need weekly sessions in which to complain about how wet you get; you

just use an umbrella, and it's taken care of. If road-
work is blocking your normal route to the office, you
don't stand on the sidewalk and whine to the pass-
ersby or wait by the side of the road for the work to
be finished; you take another route.

Similarly, if a physical task is complex, you break
it down into small steps—excruciatingly small steps.
If your entire house is a pigpen, you tackle it one
room at a time. If clearing any given room seems to
be an overwhelming task, then you break that down,
too; for example, you start cleaning the dining room
by taking all the dirty glasses to the kitchen. There,
that's done. You don't look at the whole enterprise,
feel overwhelmed, throw up your hands in surrender,
and head out the door, hoping that the cleaning fair-
ies will take care of the mess before you return.

The same is true with psychological tasks. If your
relationship problems are overwhelming, determine
what your first small step should be, focus solely on
that, and then take it. Perhaps it is just to tell your
partner that your feelings are hurt. Perhaps you
need to buy a few large suitcases and let your mother
know you'll be arriving soon. Whatever the step is—
tentative or radical—you know what you need to do.
If you don't, it's probably because you're allowing
the enormity of the task to paralyze you. Take your
attention off the big picture and concentrate on the
first action to take, the first small step.

You've developed a bad emotional habit, which
is based on the fact that you've never pushed your
brain to the next step. Maybe the result you want
isn't possible, but at least if you take the next step,
you can physically drag your mind out of the muddy
rut in which it's been wallowing. You'll be amazed

how creative you become once you force yourself to begin the process.

Thus, rather than just hearing yourself say in your head, "I don't like who I am, I want to be better, more liked, more balanced" and then stopping, keep going: "I have to take steps to figure out how to like myself, how to have more friends, how to feel like an entire and passionate person. Maybe this will take time, but I'll take small steps."

ASSIGNMENT

Take a goal that seems unattainable and write twenty-five of the smallest steps possible to get there. For example:

Goal: I want to move out.

Steps: I will . . .

1. Research neighborhoods.

2. Find out how much a rental is these days.

3. Examine my finances.

4. Start cleaning up.

5. Begin to organize my possessions.

6. Decide what I want to take with me.

7. Take unwanted things to a thrift shop.

8. Get boxes.

9. Find out if I can change my address online without having to go to the post office.

10. Make a list of friends who could help me move.

Stop complaining that your goal is so special and complex, so earth-shattering and death-defying that you can't reach it. This is negative, self-defeating thinking. You can accomplish your goal. It doesn't make it less special because you break down the challenge into small, seemingly unimaginative components; it just makes the process of change more manageable and attainable. Change your cognitions about it ("It is within my reach and control"), and your behavior will change ("Here is my first step"). Be rational, reasonable, and practical. It's not romantic or dramatic, but it will get you off the pity pot and put your goal within reach. Go—now.

ASSIGNMENT

Ask yourself the following tough questions:

- When am I misinterpreting my faith or spirituality, hoping that something will change from without? (Possible answer: I need to utilize that faith or spirituality to draw strength from within in order to make plans.)

- Do I have an objective that won't show immediate results but that I believe will produce change over time?

- When is my loyalty to someone or something getting in the way?

Q and A

Q. I started therapy figuring that it would be something like confession, that I could say everything I know I did wrong and somehow feel better. It is so much more work than I imagined. Does it get easier?

A. Yes, it does. Although you expected admit-repent, admit-repent, you are learning that it's about seeing the patterns in your behavior and figuring out why you get into these situations, what makes you repeat them, what secondary motives you have in maintaining them, and what kind of a plan you need to break the cycle, if that is your goal. Bravo for having the courage to continue despite it being so much harder than you thought. With this in mind, you might want to go back to the beginning chapters in the near future to work through this book again. *Get a Grip* is a template that you can personalize. You'll come back with a better sense of the "why," then you'll work through the chapters in order to heal, organize, eradicate, and, ultimately, have the freedom to react differently.

Q. I know it sounds like an excuse, but it really is my parents' fault that I am in this mess.

A. That may be the right reason, but simple blame without a decision to take responsibility for your life from today forward gets you nowhere. If you were in therapy, your therapist wouldn't simply tell you what you are doing wrong, because you have to keep doing your crazy little psychological tap dance until you get over being angry at Mom and Dad, or you have to bore yourself with the same sad story, until *you* are ready to change. Part of you wants to just wallow in the "it's all their fault"; everyone does this, with *they* being the boss, siblings, institutions like high school, or situations like divorce. You want to blame it on "them" and go on about being misunderstood or insisting that life is unfair and you got the short end of the stick.

You can always find excuses, whether or not they're true. "It's not that simple," you complain. "You had to be there, it was infuriating!" It's the same whether you are talking about your lousy job, your nagging boss, your horrible childhood, or your bad marriage. Get a move on: build a sculpture of "them" and burn it, do a liver cleanse (the liver is related to anger, according to Chinese medicine), then start taking steps to clear up the mess that "they" created, because "they" won't do it and it's stinking up *your* backyard.

Q. I've been writing, and believe it or not, I have been sort of surprised at how much I actually know that I wasn't aware of. Doesn't that sound funny? I mean, it's my life and body, and I've been here the whole time. Do people ever say that to you about this process?

A. Yes, often. One of my favorite quotes is from Benjamin Spock: "Trust yourself. You know more than you think you do." It's true.

Q. I used to try to convince myself that I had chosen an unconventional path, that I was marching to the beat of my own drummer or maybe that I had an irreverent wild streak. Recently, when I looked at what I have, compared to my peers, all I could see were holes in the fabric. Even trying to convince myself that I was happier than they were wasn't working anymore. The idea that I might be average and unsure of my life seems more real and more frightening than ever before. Questioning myself has actually led me to feel worse than ever before. Is this normal?

A. This is a breakthrough, when you realize that a belief you held about yourself doesn't work anymore. Unfortunately, it doesn't feel so good, does it? In therapy, you would be made to feel safe and supported as you cracked this facade. Even as you put your head down and walk against the wind, keep writing about every feeling you have, and you'll get through the storm and come out on the other side. Make sure that you have family and friends to support you during this time. Ease up on yourself, remember to take deep breaths, and reach out to your support network as you do this very important work.

DAY NINE

One Step Forward, Two Steps Back: The Mechanics of Change

Yesterday's assignments were meant to help you concretize your goals and formulate a plan that lets you reevaluate and reorganize them from ideas buzzing in your head to a sturdy infrastructure that becomes a functional framework in your life. It's a way to net, pull in, and line up those dreams and wishes that you might have deemed too idealistic.

Concretizing is where most people falter: On the one hand, they set the bar too high, fail, and become disappointed, which feeds into the notion that they should be content with where they are or, even worse, that they are

125

incapable of changing. On the other hand, steps that are too small lead to boredom, distraction, or discouragement, because the pot of gold seems so far away.

Perhaps they've faltered because they haven't gotten the stumbling blocks out of the way yet. You can walk out after a therapy session feeling confident and clearheaded only to find out later that the nagging themes that beleaguered you before are still blocking your way. It's frustrating.

Realize that therapy isn't always linear; each session doesn't necessarily build on top of the last, moving you steadily on to the next phase. Often it advances in little jolts and spurts. At other times it resembles a trek that's two steps forward, one step back. I often hear patients say, "I felt great when I left. I was clear on the steps I had to take, and I was determined. Then I got home and sort of forgot what I was supposed to do. I kind of lost my nerve or my focus."

Just as in therapy, in this chapter we'll double back, just a little, so that subsequently you can move forward more rapidly. It's like one of those refresher classes in which you review all the main topics covered so far, just to make sure that everyone is up to speed. If you think that you aren't progressing as fast as you should, you probably haven't cleared the way enough.

For instance, when you impulsively decide you'd like to be more organized, you sweep everything that's on top of your messy desk into a drawer. Close the drawer, and it looks pretty good. Then five minutes later, when you need a pen or a paper clip, you open the drawer and it's a huge hassle because you have pencils mixed up with dried-up pens, all of which are tangled up with rubber bands and paper clips. You have good intentions, you keep your eye on your goal, then before long you feel overwhelmed and defeated before you start. Once again, you are immobilized by not having done the groundwork, and you're back to square one.

What exactly is the stuff that's clogging and cluttering up your life and holding you back? Find out in the usual way: by writing down everything that comes to mind, because the answer is there. The journaling you've been doing in this process is the mirror.

Yesterday and today, you realized that you have some cleaning up to do. There are snags in the way, those *but*s and *if*s, the unknowns that have kept you dithering and stalling. Look at yesterday's list. Many of the tasks you listed you could in fact complete and cross off, but you make some kind of excuse: you don't have time for them right now; your life is complicated; you have some *other* clearing out to do first. The point yesterday was not just to have a good plan and well-defined steps; it was to see what stuff is in the way that you haven't dealt with yet.

Breaking It Down

First let's talk more about the mechanics of change. Technically, how does your brain change its mind, alter its tack, and click over to another channel? Do you ever hesitate to change your mind because you think it's a sign of weakness or a self-defeating step backward? Do you stick to your guns no matter what signals you're getting? In order for you to step forward toward change, does every detail have to be in place, organized and categorized beforehand? Does everyone have to agree that it's a good decision, or can there be a subtle hint of information to the contrary?

What about the opposite case: does any new information have you bolting in a different direction? When you do move, are you sprinting wildly or shuffling along begrudgingly? What about emotional change? Do you function the same way? Think about a situation in which you had to change emotionally. What was it like? What held you back, and what propelled you forward?

How do you deal with change in your life? Is your reaction positive or negative? If your boss tells you that he's going to make some changes, if your significant other suggests some changes to improve your relationship, or if your best friend says that she wants to tell you about a big change in her life, do you brace yourself or lean forward? Do you immediately become worried? Excited? Intrigued?

The word *change* does not have an inherently positive or negative association. You are the one who colors it. Do you automatically dig in your heels? Do you look for the positive in any situation? Do you feel left out of the decision-making process? Do you become starry-eyed and fantasize what even bigger better things are in store? Or do you start looking for the nearest exit?

Now, most important, what do you have to do in order to make the desired change flow easily and be permanent? Which "ducks" have you lined up to make sure you're on the right track? You know how to do this with other people: you choreograph the conversation so it seems to your boss that he came up with the idea; you present an option to your spouse that is good for everyone in the family, not just for you; you suggest when to have dinner to make sure you're on time for the movie afterward. Now it's time to do it for yourself. Get your pencil, pen, or computer ready; it's time to start working again.

ASSIGNMENT

1. Think of a specific behavior or situation that you want to change but still haven't taken the necessary steps to get moving. How would

you, if you were sitting across from yourself, encourage yourself to change? At what point do you start making excuses, saying, "Yes, but . . ."? Speaking to yourself in the second person, write several arguments that you would present to make this change attractive and viable.

2. Once you are convinced that this change is within your grasp, think about what else would have to happen to make you take the first step. Write down the things you would have to shift, get rid of, or figure out in order to take more of the steps you identified yesterday.

As I mentioned before, patients often stop progressing in therapy once they get to a certain level of understanding, know what their diagnostic label is, comprehend why they are grieving, and become aware of why they are discontented. They discover that recognizing the cause of their discontent or angst is enough to make them feel a bit better. They think that they now possess a complete list of practical steps that lead to change. However, there's a nagging thought of some issue that hasn't been addressed yet, and it's still blocking the way.

Let's look one more time at some old junk you haven't dealt with yet. For change to occur, you may have to work through problems or heal from a physical or emotional injury that occurred in your past. Maybe you have to finally come to terms with how deeply or insidiously your father's alcoholism affected you, how much your neglectful or self-involved mother frustrated and loaded you with repressed anger, or how a sadistic older brother kept you from feeling safe enough to express yourself as a child. It could be a specific event, an accident that still pops up in your nightmares, your parents' divorce, a debilitating injury in high school, or something else that brought you great pain or shame. Regardless of what it is, you are aware—whether from watching daytime television or from a family therapy session you were dragged to—that you have to work through the experience in order to heal and move on. So you sign up.

This is where things get tricky. You're at the point where you understand what that person, situation, or experience did to you, but then you come to a dead end. You mistakenly think, "Well, now I understand why I am the way I am, and that is the working through that makes up most of the healing, right?" No, that's not right, but it's not your fault that you think this. Remember the movie *Good Will Hunting*, in which the main character remembers the abuse he underwent and acknowledges it, and voilà, he has therapeutic success?

In real life that's when the healing would *start*; then would come the hard work of changing his current behavior related to the abuse. We are talking about lots of therapy sessions that don't make for good movies. Admitting, breaking down, crying, and understanding are *parts* of the process, but there is more to do. That is why I say that understanding is overrated. I say this in therapy repeatedly, and I frequently get back a puzzled "Huh?"

Don't get me wrong; understanding is without a doubt a very important step. I do have my patients examine, pore over, and dissect the roots and causes of their discomforts in order to encourage discussion and to shake them up, especially if they have become complacent or numb from years of thinking that understanding (that is, being able to put labels on their anxieties or distress) is the cure-all and now find themselves frustrated by the lack of change in their lives.

What is great about today's exercises is that you just have to do them the way you'd pop a vitamin pill. You really don't have to become scientific or obsessive about them. (If you do, however, that's great.) Go through the motions, being as open-minded as you can, even if you don't understand how they're working. Sometimes you just take cold medicine, not really understanding how it makes you sniffle less, don't you? Just knowing that it does work ultimately makes you feel better.

Even though therapy is about thinking and processing, there are times when you don't have to fully understand the theories, notions, concepts, or beliefs involved. Some feelings and experiences are beyond words (love and soul mates are concepts that are hard to explain)—that is why art therapy and dance therapy work. Maybe words have helped you to get to 85 percent, but that other 15 percent, which defies logic and grammar, is holding you back. You can't seem to get a handle on it, so you stall. Feel my hand on your back giving you a figurative push. Let's keep going and move on to the next section, your metaphor.

Creating Your Metaphor

"My metaphor? What in the world is my metaphor?" you ask. Let me give you a hand with this. You want to find a symbolic and physical equivalent of what you want to do.

Does this seem to have a feng shui kind of feeling to it? Here are some examples to make the concept clearer: If you want to slow down, think tai chi; if you want to become motivated and speed up, think spin class. You have to put your imagination in gear and visualize the change metaphorically. Hold on to this concept and keep reading.

Let's say you're working on getting out of a relationship. You've become glued to the other person in an unhealthy way, and you want to break free. Find something that represents freedom to you, perhaps a physical representation of what you want to do, such as getting unstuck. Have you ever tried line dancing? You dance with one person for a few seconds, and before you know it, you're on to the next. You don't have time to become attached to anyone; it's a continual process of moving together and then moving away, so this kind of dance is a physical representation of breaking connections. It's corny, you think. That's tough. Do it—doctor's orders.

Right now you have to act as the therapist who would make the metaphoric suggestions and then say to yourself, "Just try it." It's effortless, because, in a sense, you are doing the homework someone else has given you. Let's make it even easier on you. I am telling you to do it. Find the wackiest, out-there metaphor and put your heart into it. "Okay," you sigh, "but give me some more examples; I still don't get it."

When patients become stuck here, I tell them the story behind Burning Man—a huge festival that takes place in the Nevada desert every summer. A man who had been dumped by his girlfriend started a party at which he would burn a scarecrow that represented the man for whom she left him. The party grew bigger and bigger. Last year forty-seven thousand people attended. I think you've got the picture now. On with the writing.

ASSIGNMENT

1. Find a metaphor for your change. You don't have to understand it fully—just create it. Be supercreative, get wild, be silly, and go over the top.
2. Write about the experience.
3. Write about the process in excruciating detail; do the therapy part yourself.

It would take another three or four chapters, or perhaps an entire book, to examine and explain why this exercise works, and why these two things—the metaphor and the physical equivalent—help to heal you and get you unstuck. You can read and philosophize on your own, because I'm not here to convince you why this works; I'm here to tell you that it does and to encourage you to get down to business by applying it specifically to you and your life.

There are two steps to take here, and they seem to be opposites: one is metaphorical or creative, and the other is more experiential and practical. You need to do both. Let's put it this way: You feel yourself coming down with a cold, so you go to the kitchen and get some tea and vitamin C, then you go the bathroom and grab the decongestant. You turn on the humidifier, slather Vicks VapoRub on your chest, maybe take some echinacea or another herb, and finally, you go to bed early.

This is an example of putting together everyone's advice. No matter how you felt, Grandma always brewed you some kind of tea. Your doctor is always urging, "Hydrate, hydrate, hydrate." Vitamin C and echinacea, you know, have something to do with colds. Vicks—well, your mom always did that for you when you were a child, so it's mostly habit. The humidifier? That was what your cousin recommended the last time you were sick, and it seemed to help.

No matter what problem you are grappling with, there is some healing to be done. I wish there were another word, because *healing* is a bit overused. It pops up in every sitcom. Let's search for other phrases: Maybe there are things you need to put in order? Get closure on? Put to rest? Make right some bad choices? Even if you don't have an overwhelming issue that is looming threateningly over you, you can surely find one that has been nagging at you.

As a psychologist, I take a very holistic approach. I say let's attack this problem from all sides. Let's use Eastern, Western, New Age, Jungian, and folklore techniques and advice. Use whatever you are into: tea leaf readings, aromatherapy, fortune cookies. Then add your gut instincts and my clinical intuition, and let's move on to the next chapter.

Q and A

Q. In doubling back in order to go forward, what is the very first step?

A. Awareness. Sometimes you feel out of sorts, you have a medical problem that doesn't resolve, you can't sleep, or you just feel bummed out. Figuring out what is at the root of the issue, when it started, and why it began is the first step toward change. All the previous chapters of this book have been set up to help you to find awareness.

Q. What is your favorite saying about change?

A. Mahatma Gandhi once said, "Be the change you want to see in the world."

Q. How will I know what changes I need to make?

A. Becoming psychologically minded, insightful, and evolved all come from asking yourself the questions posed in this text and completing the assignments with intent and honesty. The awareness you have mined from days 1 through 8 has shifted your perspective and expectations, regardless of how far you've moved the boulders or blocks out of your way. The changes that you need to have happen will become more apparent, as if you called them to come out in some way. You should no longer believe that clarity about what you should be doing is completely elusive.

Q. I have a list of life goals, a to-do list for the year that I make every New Year. Is that helpful?

A. Yes, but I want you to try something new. I bet you are very familiar with the last couple of items on your to-do list that you transfer every year to a new list, aren't you? Maybe such an item is apologizing to a friend, making amends, righting a wrong, visiting a grave, or paying off a loan. Maybe it's throwing out your hidden binge food, ripping up a phone number, or going to your first AA meeting. Turn the list upside down. Pick number 10 or number 9 to do first—today. You just cringed—I saw you. From your reaction, I gather that such an item is not at the bottom of the list by chance. Why are you avoiding this specific one?

Q. I'm having difficulty finding a metaphor for my change. Help!

A. One of my patients wanted to be more assertive, more vocal. She found a karaoke bar that had small private rooms and sang her heart out. She was terrible, she admitted, but it was really cathartic and started the momentum of her being heard and expressing herself. I was on *The Rachael Ray Show* once, talking about the new trend of divorce parties, when one of the audience members reported making a small coffin for her wedding ring when she got divorced. It helped her to heal—and she turned the idea into a business!

A popular but very misguided example of this approach is women who want to slim down and buy jeans they want to be able to fit into someday. Most of my dieting patients found that this eventually frustrated them rather than inspired them to lose weight. If thinking of a different word is helpful, think ritual. Rituals are very important; we don't have enough of them, and we don't spend enough time doing them. Parties, ceremonies, and memorials are all in that vein.

DAY TEN

Myths, Lies, and Straight-Out Silliness

You love top-ten, top-five, or top-three lists—the best, worst, most popular, or biggest-secret lists that provide summaries and cut-to-the-chase information. This chapter features a top-seven list: seven psychological myths or misunderstandings that interfere with the therapeutic progress. They are what patients come to therapy believing in wholeheartedly; the ideas they live by, make decisions by, and, worst of all, don't question.

At least one of these is definitely in your repertoire. It might not be a principle that you preach openly; it may, instead, be somewhat subtle or insidious or be something that feels more like a superstition than a deep belief, but it affects the way you make decisions. So read each myth carefully, paying close attention and really checking in with yourself. Then, when you move on to the assignments, you'll rip the misinformation to shreds.

1. *Myth:* Whatever you think about, you attract.

   - *Truth:* The oversimplified idea that you attract what you think about, good or bad, has been called the Law of Attraction. A more sophisticated and effective way to think about this concept is that you need to visualize what you want and then take the necessary steps to get there. Of course, this realistic definition is less magical than the more popular one, but it is also less dangerous, because you'll plan for worst-case scenarios rather than just trying to avoid them.

   - *In therapy:* In addition to brainstorming and supporting patients as they move toward their goals, I ask about all the possible outcomes—on a spectrum. "What's the worst that could happen?" is easier to consider in therapy because the therapy room is a neutral place; patients feel safe talking about the consequence of their actions without superstitiously fearing that they are bringing it down upon themselves. This is important for the following reason: When you block out a thought or ignore it, it unconsciously festers deep inside you and becomes ominous, bigger than you, and very, very threatening. Being able to talk about the worst outcome puts the situation in perspective, however. You see that it isn't as overwhelming as you imagined. You realize that you can come up with a plan of action or be more flexible in your expectations of the outcome.

- *What to do:* Plan practical steps to achieve what you want, and think about the range of possible outcomes, including the worst that could happen; then plan accordingly. Don't obsess about the bad, building it up and making yourself suffer; just troubleshoot. By contemplating the worst-case scenario and taking the necessary preventive measures, you will be better prepared *if* it happens. Once you've done this, visualize what you'd like to take place, and then put ten times as much energy into making that happen.

2. *Myth:* Therapy is a place to be hugged and coddled.

    - *Truth:* Some people mistakenly think that therapy is for the weak or the really nutty or that it is a cushy process in which you'll soothingly be told that everything is going to be okay. On some days you may indeed be hugged in therapy—either literally, if your therapist is the huggy type, or metaphorically, when you receive positive feedback. However, it's not always this way.

    - *In therapy:* In good therapy, you will at times feel gut-wrenching confusion, question everything you've believed, and strain your brain trying to find a new definition for yourself. You'll often yearn for the times you were just *moderately* confused and less introspective, and you'll wish you could go back to those days. Ultimately, you become aware of the great number of choices you have, and you stop going along in life just reacting to every situation thoughtlessly.

    - *What to do:* Stretch yourself and push your limits in order to think outside the box. The assignments are set up to help you to do this. Thinking in new and unusual ways is tiring, but moving out of your comfort zone is necessary when you're looking for change. You might stumble and even trip—hard. Someone once explained to me, "If you try to do a headstand or a handstand and you fall, at least you were where you wanted to be for a split second, which is closer than hopping around cautiously in an attempt to get there and never making it at all." So try overshooting. Even if you fall, keep in mind that you were at the point of success, if only for a split second. Maybe next time it will be two seconds, and longer the time after that. We'll talk about this in practical terms later. For now, just understand the concept.

3. *Myth:* Therapy has to include dramatic screaming and crying breakthroughs to be effective.

   • *Truth:* Some of the biggest psychological breakthroughs are very, very quiet. It's ironic that the biggest eureka moments may happen when you are by yourself, in complete or relative silence. Patients have asked me how they will know when they have a breakthrough. Experiencing a revelatory moment in therapy is like having an orgasm: you know when you've had one. There are no maybes here. It's an "Aha!" moment: all of a sudden you realize that something really important has occurred, and it's an amazing feeling. You might blurt out the perfect solution in the middle of a brainstorming meeting, or maybe you'll notice something in your peripheral vision that saves your life. A "lightbulb moment" in therapy occurs when you realize that there is a third option you hadn't considered, and it sets you free. The feeling is one of triumph, intense relief, and surprise. All the work you are doing now may inspire change today, or it may be a catalyst that starts the momentum. Here are some signals that an "Aha!" moment has occurred for you (and, as you can see, they are all pretty quiet):

You've been shouldering a heavy responsibility for months, even years, and suddenly you realize that you aren't to blame, that you don't have to carry all the weight yourself.

You've been stuck between a rock and a hard place, and all at once a third option becomes clear that frees you.

You finally understand that you can let something or someone go and live quite happily without the perfect ending on which you'd been insisting.

- *In therapy:* In meditation and prayer, silence is essential, but in therapy it is necessary to have a dialogue with yourself. A therapist will help you to slow your thought processes down considerably so that you can learn to do this. You free-associate, ponder, brainstorm, and clear your head so you can hear yourself think. Therapy is also quiet—no cell phone, no other distractions—and your therapist will let you pause as long as you want before you answer (something you might never have in real life, given the pressure to answer confidently or fill an uncomfortable silence in a social situation). Think about how much noise there is around you all the time: the songs while you are on hold on the telephone waiting for customer service; your cell phone buzzing that a message has come in; the music piped in overhead in every waiting room, store, or restaurant you enter; the raucous blare of a television; and that maddening voice in your computer that announces, "You've got mail!" Some people find peace and quiet only at church, on the toilet, or when drifting off to sleep. You need a little more quiet time than that to check in with yourself. You might have the solutions right on the tip of your tongue, but you have to give your mind and your soul the floor if you are going to hear them.

- *What to do:* Start with five minutes a day when you don't have anything to do but breathe and take account of how you are feeling. Don't do anything, just acknowledge. Your brain is working all the time, summarizing, coming to conclusions; if you don't give it the stillness in which to speak up, you'll never hear what it has to say. All you have to do is pause. Therefore, make yourself sit in silence every day for a short time. Be alone. Be quiet. Make yourself tolerate the quietude. Take a few deep breaths and scan your body: How is your sore shoulder? Are you hungry? Breathe deeply again. Are you still worried about something? Perhaps you have to go to the bathroom and you didn't notice until now. Then, as you learned on day 1, ask yourself how you are, listen to the answer, see if any new solutions come to mind, and repeat your Power Statement to yourself. That's it. It's brain maintenance, and it's a very important part of your emotional health.

4. *Myth:* Accepting and loving your family is the goal in therapy.

- *Truth:* There is no one-size-fits-all goal in therapy. On the subject of family, I usually hear one of two extreme responses: "I don't really need therapy; I love my mother, and my dad is a great guy" or "My mom was a floozy and my dad was a rat— there, I said it!" Okay, so they weren't the Brady Bunch or the Huxtables or any other TV family. In therapy you need to examine the role and influence of your family, but you shouldn't use it as an excuse for your adult behavior, even a tiny bit. The bottom line is that your parents birthed you. Big deal—people don't have to get a degree or even a permission slip to give birth. Don't get me wrong: I'm not saying that conception, birth, and babies aren't divine and wonderful; I'm saying that procreation is fairly common (done by all types of people, animals, plants, and bugs, either in pairs or solo). Perhaps your parents were decent and raised you lovingly, or perhaps they were terrible and should never have had the right to raise even chickens. No matter what the conditions were in which you were conceived, born, and raised, it's done and you're here.

- *In therapy:* As a therapist, I do want you to talk about how you dealt with your parents when you were a vulnerable little child. If you have an issue with them now, you're more likely to be able to say, "Excuse me, Dad, but the way you belittle Mom is affecting my definition of love and relationships. You have to stop that right now." You'd protect yourself: "Mom, you are being irrational, so I am going to go for a run and I'll be back later." When you were a child, however, you were at their mercy and could not respond to or challenge them in this way.

- *What to do:* Now you are an adult, and you know that you can do what you want without your dad grounding you. Convincing your brain and your soul of this is a lot harder, but just telling yourself that you have choices is an important first step. It is certainly hard work to undo all their negative effects (subtle or serious, big scars or small) on you, but you *can* rewire yourself. Start to think about the people you were given as a family, and accept that it was a random happening; it wasn't logical or necessarily meant to be, and you didn't choose them. It's not your fault. Now you are all grown up and have work to do—whether it's a tweak or an overhaul.

5. *Myth:* You only have one chance to change your life.

- *Truth:* There is always time to clean up your act. Many people love this myth because it gives them the excuse not to face up to the tough issues. They tell themselves that they should have done it when they were younger, when they had time to themselves, before they were married, and so on. The moment to do something about it has passed, they believe; oh well, where's the remote?

- *In therapy:* I assure patients that they don't have only one chance to fix something or else the opportunity is gone forever. Problems will surface repeatedly and unexpectedly until you fix them. An unresolved issue will keep reappearing in different guises until you really understand the cause and address the problem differently. To use a tennis metaphor, life will keep serving the ball to you the same way until you learn a new way to hit it back.

- *What to do:* Next time you are in the same old troublesome situation, examine it carefully. There you go again, having a "misunderstanding" with someone. Here's that state of affairs in which you end up feeling like the victim once again. You really thought this boyfriend would be different, but he's exactly like the others. Rather than just being relieved when the unpleasant situation is over, look it in the eye. Walk around it and examine it from all angles. Stop reacting the same way; try a different way and see if the outcome is different. Is your current approach to a certain situation not working? Is the way you are reacting or understanding something not correct? Don't worry if you can't do it this time; life will hand it to you again, in a different form, until you get it. Be determined to try something new. Keep in mind that there has to be a better way than simply repeating the same old reaction and hoping for a better outcome. Keep in mind Albert Einstein's definition of insanity: doing the same thing over and over and expecting a different result. You're not crazy, so, if necessary, recruit your friends to help you. Tell them the following: "The next time you hear me say this, or if you ever see me do that, throw a bucket of cold water on me or take me by the shoulders and shake me."

6. *Myth:* You must be intensely and exclusively focused on your inner world and deepest thoughts in order to get what you need from therapy.

   • *Truth:* You do have to be introspective, but at some point you should go in the opposite direction to get a breath of fresh air. You will need to switch off and do something else for a while. Therapy work makes you focus intently on the details of your life and reactions, but you need a balance.

- *In therapy:* Patients often ask me why I advise them to "get out of their heads" ("But doc, I've been trying to get deeper and deeper into my head!"). I tell them this when I notice that they need a reality check, when they need perspective on how small their problems are compared to those of the rest of the world.

- *What to do:* Make sure you can go in and out of both realms. At times you should take yourself seriously, and at other times you should laugh at yourself. This will allow you to have some perspective and realize that although whatever you are going through is difficult and painful, there are people who are in worse straits. Going back and forth like this—listening to yourself intently, then getting a grip and knowing that you'll live—may sound strange to you, but realizing that you can do this will give you the ability to let yourself rest and "percolate" for a while when you need to do so.

7. *Myth:* Understanding is the number one goal of therapy.

- *Truth:* Understanding is overrated; change doesn't necessarily follow understanding. We are stubborn, habit-loving animals. Many patients stop as soon as they understand why they do something; they give it a name and then allow themselves to continue doing it. I mentioned this in an earlier chapter, but it deserves to be said twice.

- *In therapy:* Just because you now know *why* you are unhappy (or overeat or sabotage relationships or feel unfulfilled) doesn't mean that the work stops there. Many people come to a grinding halt because the understanding gives them control and an excuse to sit back. Knowing that you are commitment-phobic, have abandonment issues, are codependent, or have a history of alcoholism doesn't mean that this is as good as it gets. Unfortunately, your brain is set up to undergo the least possible change, to keep you at just "good enough." Change takes effort: your brain muscles become sore, you don't want to revisit some memories, or you might have to tolerate being lonely or confused for a while.

- *What to do:* Acknowledge that moving to the next level of work can make you anxious because all of the ingrained patterns of behavior from childhood are being questioned and shuffled. Take a look at days 8 and 9 again. Check in with yourself, pat yourself on the back, repeat your power statement, and take a deep breath.

ASSIGNMENT

Write down a brief reaction to each of the following questions:

- Which of the seven myths surprised you the most? ("Wow! I thought that was absolutely true.")
- Which one is the most popular belief among your friends? ("Everyone I know believes that.")
- Which one did you know was only a myth? ("I never believed that!")
- Which one do you need to work on?

Now expand on your answers, especially the last one.

ASSIGNMENT

Write several worst-case scenarios that keep you from taking action. Then step back and ask yourself if what you fear would *really* happen. Do a reality check. For example:

- If I moved out on my own, my mother would die. (Reality check: Would she actually keel over and die? She will die eventually—so will you and so will I—but probably not because you signed a lease on a place a few blocks away.)

- If I got a divorce I would be out on the street, and I'd starve. (Reality check: Good planning and savings are important for making this transition; maybe life wouldn't be as comfy, but you probably won't have to set up a little tent outside, either. You may have to downsize, but in the long run it will be a good trade-off.)

- If she left me, I couldn't go on living. (Reality check: You were living before you met her, remember?)

- If I quit my job I'll never find another one. (Reality check: Although times are tough and a lot depends on where you live, if you really need a job, are open minded, and have a good work ethic, *never* is a bit of an exaggeration.)

Keep on bringing up fears about making a change, and write them down. Phrasing them as questions invites your unconscious to provide commonsense answers. An unexamined fear is always a lot scarier than an examined one. Scrutinize it carefully; take it apart, strand by strand. When you look at the worst-case scenarios head-on, you'll usually see that the situation isn't really as bad as you thought.

ASSIGNMENT

Write down all of the times you have experienced the same issue in different guises. How many significant others have started out being supportive and loving and ended up nagging you constantly? Who was the first person like that? Who was the last? Who was the umpteenth one in between? Write about them; seek the common denominators. Your repeated experience isn't about uncanny bad luck or fate; inevitably, there's one big common denominator: you! Write about what you're doing that is attracting this kind of person, whether a boss or a bedmate.

ASSIGNMENT

Now write about the actions you have to take to make change happen. Visualize the concrete steps you are going to take that will lead to the right man, woman, or job, even if at this moment it seems to be beyond your reach. Can you specify what you would have to do to be happier, more self-reliant, or more assertive? Don't hold back: write the things that seem impossible for someone like you to do. Now is not the time to censor yourself; go off on tangents, push the envelope. If you feel yourself becoming cynical and sarcastic, call yourself on it and refocus.

Q and A

Q. You said to make sure that I am specific about what I want. What should I do if what I want is somewhat abstract or even impossible?

A. You want to be taller, have fewer children, or go back in time. The problem with being in that state is that you get used to the feeling of just wishing. Pining is part of the process, and you are almost comfortable in pine mode. You yearn, yearn, and yearn—and, frankly, you've become a bit of a martyr. Therefore, mourn that you can't go back in time, write about self-pity, then come up with a new plan. Maybe the plan includes heel lifts and a shorter partner, or maybe the solution is to send your children to a summer camp that is out of cell-phone range. Be assertive about problem solving.

Q. Can you give me more examples of practicing, of getting over fear, and of shaking things up a bit in my brain?

A. One of my favorite books is *The 4-Hour Work Week*. Author Tim Ferriss recommends that a man ask every woman at a shopping mall for her telephone number in order to get over that fear, and he suggests lying down on the floor in a public place to shake your brain up. Try not to get arrested, but be creative and have a sense of humor about it all.

Q. I'm trying to focus on my goal with intention, be proactive in moving that way, and make sure that I have plans in case it doesn't go my way. Is that is the right thing to do?

A. Yes, but there is one more thing. It's limiting to fixate on only one form of success without thinking about the range of possibilities you have. How often has something not gone "your way," but after time has passed you are grateful that it didn't, because it somehow saved you from something you didn't know at the time?

Q. I'm still digesting the last chapter and this one, but what is a concept that I should really understand by now?

A. Gaining awareness is a subtle concept that is priceless. Just being aware of how you feel, realizing how long you've felt that way, and understanding that it's not a sentence you have to live with gives you so many more choices than you ever envisioned. You can't put it up on your fridge or even frame it, but it's huge that you can acknowledge that your story, your soul, and your psyche are much more complex than you ever envisioned. Congratulations. (Insert virtual-therapist hug here.)

DAY ELEVEN

Somewhere over the Rainbow?

"I *just* want to be happy." It's a simple sentence that I hear time and again from people sitting in front of me on the couch. They emphasize *just* as if talking about a parking space, privacy while showering, or a stamp for a piece of mail. "It's really not too much to ask for! I *just* want to be happy." These people assume that happiness is a natural state and that everyone else is already there—at the unlimited open bar, hors d'oeuvres passing by. For them, however, figuring out what happiness is and how to achieve it is baffling. They feel sure that they have been denied the "pursuit of happiness" that is mentioned in the Declaration of Independence.

Maybe as you are reading the word *happiness*, you are thinking, "Great—finally, an easy day in this two-week crash course from hell." Then you say, "I know what *happy* is," and you envision a fat, jocular dwarf in *Snow White and the Seven Dwarfs*. Sorry—although the word *happiness* may conjure up images of this sort, that isn't quite what I mean. Nor will the work today be a picnic for you.

When was the last time you were *truly* happy? Faced with that question, you might pause, look at your nails, and scratch your head. "When the Red Sox beat the Yankees in 2004," you venture; or possibly, "My honeymoon, maybe?" Perhaps you think about a vacation a few years ago when you were stretched out on the beach, margarita in hand, listening to the house band playing "Hot, Hot, Hot" for the fifth time, and musing, "Life's pretty darn good." What about last week, this week, and today?

Too many adults believe that happiness is a luxury, that if they are *too* happy they aren't working hard enough. They've run out of experiences in which they feel content or blissful for purely personal reasons. They have reached the point at which they don't even have original moments of happiness to call to mind. When they describe what happiness is, they sound like an ad for a new car or an imported beer. Maybe it's even sadder: happiness, for them, is merely a lack of stress.

Let's start by coming up with other words for *happy*, just to increase your chances of identifying those moments. Since the word *happy* may evoke images of clowns and cupcakes, think about terms that tend to be more "adult" in content: *satisfied, contented, enthusiastic, pleased, delighted, ecstatic.* When you say the word *happy*, bring to mind these words instead; it will make this lesson easier and more meaningful. Over the years patients have given me quite a variety of definitions of the term *happy*. Do any of these resonate with you?

- "Having free time makes me happy—knowing that I've gotten everything done and that what I have is 'me' time. No one needs anything from me."

- "When my day is going my way—smoothly, without a glitch. Everyone is pleasant, for once. I'm not hitting any walls."

- "Doing things I feel passionate about, when I am really living life to the fullest."

- "Seeing my kids happy makes me happy. Their smiling and laughing brings out the best feeling in me."

- "When I have a moment in which I feel talented at my job. I've done a project well at work and I realize that I am good at what I do."

- "When I have the impression that the world is a decent place, when I am not worrying and I believe that people are intrinsically good."

- "When I'm learning something—anything, from a new recipe to snowboarding. When I'm inspired or excited by something."

- "When I feel really connected to my friends or family—feeling loved by them."

- "Feeling independent and self-sufficient makes me happy."

ASSIGNMENT

Holding on to your present definition of the word *happy*, write down at least five instances in the past week when you were feeling truly happy. It could have been a millisecond; the length of time doesn't matter. Be specific and generous with details.

As you look at your list, you may come to the conclusion that the definition of happiness is unbelievably subjective and that ultimately it *is* elusive. There can't be a one-size-fits-all kind of happiness.

Nevertheless, when you start grappling with the question of what happiness is and what it actually means to you, and then seek to determine if you are truly happy, you have taken a big step. You have gone past the little and at times petty annoyances that you examined in earlier chapters and are now peering deep into the well of your soul and asking what might be a disquieting question.

You are not being sidetracked by the sitcoms' or soap operas' portrayal of happiness. The idea of "priceless" from the credit card commercial may not be a good fit for you. Maybe happiness for you means camera-flash short moments of just feeling calm, or it could be an entire hour when you aren't "John, the bartender" anymore but instead are "Juan, the salsa dancer," and it only happens once a week, Wednesday at 7:30 p.m. At least you have grabbed some happiness. Don't let go.

Don't worry if you still don't have a fifty-words-or-less definition of happiness. Real happiness has nothing to do with a bank account, a place to which you finally arrive, or the number of friends' names in your address book. It is *you* who has the ultimate control over attaining and holding on to happiness, and that is what this chapter is about.

I know you are thinking, "That's a nice concept, Dr. B., but I don't have any instructions on specifically what to do. Give me the recipe." We'll get there. For now, just think a moment about how much time you spend *postponing* happiness, believing that it will come *later*: after you finish one more semester, after you get out of this job, after you find your soul mate, after you get over an injury, after you reach a certain weight, after all the paperwork is done, after someone apologizes for some terrible thing. That is a lot of waiting. You'd better have an iPod or a good book with you.

Let's go back to your definition of happiness. Is there a difference between being a happy grown-up and being a happy child, or can happy grown-ups be childlike? Many patients describe being happy as being playful and silly, as they were in childhood. For adults, the definition seems to be more about *not* being worried, *not* being stressed; it sounds more like the absence of something. It often sounds closer to being relaxed. Do any of the following "nots" sound familiar to you?

Happiness is:

- Not having to worry about money
- Not being pressured
- Not being alone
- Not having a stressful job
- Not being anxious about the kids
- Not being concerned about aging parents
- Not being dependent on others
- Not agonizing over everyday decisions
- Not being scared

ASSIGNMENT

Make your own list of "nots," building on the above, if necessary.

I find it interesting that when patients bring up the theme of happiness in therapy, the first thing they do is talk about others: "Well, he looks happy.

Why? What is he doing right?" Implicit in this is self-criticism, the idea that the patient is doing something wrong. However, you never really know exactly what happens when that "happy guy" goes home and closes the door, what goes through his mind before he goes to sleep, what he's feeling when he turns off the light and is alone in the dark.

As part of your journey of self-discovery, it is necessary to understand that outwardly happy and inwardly happy are two very different things. The first rule is to stop comparing yourself to others. Happiness is the most personally defined topic there is, even more so than what constitutes good sex or beauty.

As you think about yourself being happy, be wary of comparisons that creep into your mind. Set your own bar and make your own classification. "How in the world do I do that?" you ask. Calm down—you already know. Do the work and devote the time you need for writing about happiness—you know how to do this now. Once you start writing and working, you'll reach a specific definition, even if you don't think you have one now. Don't worry about it sounding profound or intense. No rhymes or haikus are necessary, either.

ASSIGNMENT

1. Chronicle specific episodes of "forced" happiness. For example, when did you first have an inkling that you were faking a smile? When did you catch yourself saying, "This pie is delicious, really incredible" when you

knew that it was mediocre, at best? It's like trying to convince the small child inside you, "Whee, aren't we having fun?" It doesn't work. Look over your list and ask yourself who was setting the bar: who was telling you to smile, to compliment the cook, to appear happy at all costs.

2. Now look at happiness from another angle: Are you sabotaging yourself? Are you actually not allowing yourself to be happy? Are you being hypercritical? Do you find yourself evaluating the moment instead of just savoring it? Write down several such incidents and see if you can zoom in on the identity of that inner killjoy who is saying, "Not bad, but it could have been better." Write about why you can't just think, "Hey, this is kinda nice." Whether you are an *American Idol* judge or a quality controller at Hasenpfeffer Incorporated, why can't you leave your job at work and just enjoy the moment?

Chasing Happiness

Realize that in today's world people are under a lot of pressure to appear happy at specific times. Sometimes the pressure to be positive is exhausting. Trying to be a person who sees the glass half full instead of half empty when you feel drained is a frustrating exercise. As a result, you are both unhappy *and* tired—a bad combination. Yet chasing happiness is something everyone does. Some people talk about happiness as if it were a tropical paradise with a free golf course and unlimited drinks. For others it is an ideal weight or a perfect job or partner. They don't have it yet; it's just over the next hill.

Admitting (and I do mean *admitting*) that you are happy at a certain moment won't ward off a better moment (if it's going to happen). The whole idea of being happy right now is simple to express but as complicated as quantum physics to put into motion. The Chinese philosopher Wu Men (whose sayings appear everywhere, from fortune cookies to the box tops of Celestial Seasonings tea) celebrates spring, summer, autumn, and winter, but he advises us to live and be happy in the present: "If your mind isn't clouded by unnecessary things, this is the best season of your life."

This means, for example, that if you clear your mind for a moment after you have finished writing and feel relieved and lighter, you might conclude that you are feeling pretty darn good today. It's about finding bite-sized pieces of happiness, then admitting that they are just enough to make you smile.

The key is to string together enough moments that you can identify as happy until you have half an hour's worth, then almost an entire day, and eventually 51 percent of the time. This means that you can then define yourself as, for the most part, a happy person: someone who is content, who experiences joy, and who is satisfied with life. Once you get to that point, everyone wants to sit next to you; they're hoping that it's contagious or that you are giving it away for free.

In simple, concrete terms, happiness can be achieved by extending moments of joy and shortening moments of pain or displeasure, whether this is achieved by your taking control of your perceptions (focusing more on the former and less on the latter) or your actually creating more minutes of happy time. Maybe you simply need to acknowledge a moment of happiness, even something as simple as enjoying great shower pressure or savoring your aunt's meat loaf.

It's interesting that two people can do exactly the same things every day yet perceive happiness so differently. One might rate her day as a 6, on a scale of 10, in terms of happiness, whereas the other gives it a 9. It's the same as defining *rich* and *poor*. Is being happy, then, about perspective, whom you are comparing yourself to, or your expectations? Much of what you feel is influenced by people around you. Sit with people who are chronic complainers—whose small talk consists of complaints about everything from the weather to the effervescence of the champagne—and the world will look bleaker. Then sit with some optimists and listen to how it's partly sunny outside rather than partly cloudy. Happiness, then, is your choice, and yours alone.

Perhaps you've done all the things that are supposed to make you happy—collecting Indian dream catchers, getting tattoos of Chinese symbols for happiness, drinking more water to detoxify—and you're still not happy. Quite often, people who come to therapy can't even put their dissatisfaction into words. Asking them to define happiness invariably yields a blank stare or a convoluted answer like "I just want to wake up and look forward to the day and feel complete and look around and somehow have things make sense, you know, feel like I am where I am supposed to be." Women and men come to me, and their eyes fill up as they say, "I'm not really sad, I'm just not happy. What is wrong with me?" Others seem baffled and finally admit, "I'm not as happy as I should be."

Let's do some work.

ASSIGNMENT

1. How often have you added up everything you've done in life, thinking, "I'm [insert your age], and is this all that I have?" At what moment have you wondered, "Is this what I am reduced to?" How about "I have *all* this, and I am *still* not happy?" Which one of these is you? Start writing, and keep going even if you catch yourself becoming dramatic. What specific events in your life do you think were formative in causing you to be unhappy? What comes to mind most quickly? A specific year? A particular person? Don't censor yourself.

2. Ask yourself, "What would it take to make me happy?" Reflect on what you wrote in response to question 1. Start very simply: "To be happy, I need . . ." Continue writing.

3. Now switch gears. Make a second column. Count all of the things you *do* have, all of the things you *can* do for which you are grateful. Your list should be at least a page long. If you haven't come to the end of the page, add details or huge general statements ("I'm losing my hair but have a well-shaped head"; "I have great teeth"; "My coworkers seem happy to see me when I arrive at work").

This isn't meant to make you feel guilty for your responses in your previous answer; it's a different question altogether. People frequently squelch their sadness and anger with guilt when instead they should explore the feelings fully in order to be able to move on to gratitude. *Now* you may reprimand yourself for not paying more attention to these gifts. Be careful, however; this doesn't make the things you listed in the first item less of a problem, but it does give you a psychological kick in the pants to gain some perspective. Acknowledge that you have to work on your definition of happiness.

Push your bottom lip out and blink (classic sad face), vent a bit, problem-solve for a minute, gain some perspective and show some gratitude, go back to problem-solving (the second item), and move yourself in that direction. This sounds simple, but it is actually full of psychological expertise and clinical knowledge that would take another chapter to explain. I have given you a straight answer; now it's your turn to delve into it.

Getting something out of the way, and over with, can make you happy; just getting from A to B can indeed be enough, so let's work on this particular and somewhat subtle aspect of happiness.

ASSIGNMENT

1. Make a list of dull or stupid things you have to do, or even just must-do things that you keep putting off, such as cleaning the incredibly dusty fan blades or getting a flu shot.

2. Look at the list. Which one of these items have you put off the longest? Do that one.

Do it right now—I'm not kidding. Then take a few seconds and be happy that you did it. The usual reaction is to say to yourself, "See, you big dummy, that wasn't so bad." This time, however, you're going to smile and give yourself some credit. Make an exercise out of thinking about how good you feel as a result. Is this "cheating" because it's not pure, organic happiness? Not at all—it's just a different flavor.

3. For the next three days grab a few minutes of happiness by completing one of the dreaded tasks.

Now I want to talk to you about the importance of playing. There are joyless people who insist that they don't have time to have fun. Believe me, that's a cop-out. They've simply forgotten how to be happy, and they don't want to admit it. When pushed, they do what they are told is fun: going to an amusement park, a comedy club, or Las Vegas. "I'm in a fun place," they say to themselves, "so I must be having fun." They go to built-in fun institutions because life has become so complicated that they now have to schedule their fun or have someone else set it up for them. Moreover, they only have a fixed amount of time, so the fun has to start right away. For three nights and four days they need to efficiently have fun. Then they have to show others that they are having fun. You know the type: "Look at me, I'm having so much fun. Whee!"

Part of you is reading and starting to recoil. First I asked you to keep smiling, and now I'm going to ask you to have fun. This is called "fun pressure." Vicarious fun is so much easier.

Much of what ruins fun is that you are constantly checking in: "Am I having fun yet, am I having fun?" Then "Am I still having fun?" "Still? No, wait, I think it's waning; ah, no—I still have some left; oh, no, not much. Ugh, all gone."

In addition, you've been so busy working, doing errands, making sure that your socks match, having your cholesterol checked and your teeth cleaned, and taking care of your child's rash. No responsible adult has too much fun, you believe. If you're doing things right, you're too busy and too tired. There's just no time to have fun if you're a working adult with a family.

I promise that I won't ask you to sing in a karaoke bar, but we do have to talk more about this excruciating topic. It's today's work, so just accept it.

ASSIGNMENT

1. Do something fun—anything. There is no need for a huge commitment; it can be something small. Promise yourself that you will do it within the next twenty-four hours. What things made you happy in the past that you have stopped doing? Horseback riding? Playing an instrument? You don't have to sign up for a twenty-four-session hustle class, but find out where there is a dance studio near you. At least do the research.

2. Do you have a not-so-fun friend or colleague who is the ultimate pessimist—someone who is sarcastic or catty or has a mean streak? Limit your time with that person. Make plans to hang out with the friend with the contagious laugh. Get out your calendar and call her right now.

3. Go back into your stream-of-conscious- ness writing and look at a particular topic in your background that relates to happiness: mourn that the episode didn't go the way you wanted, create a metaphor for it, and start doing the work. Check yourself for sabotage (recall secondary motives to not succeed), then take steps to bring the episode back into your life in the form you want.

In this chapter, you've defined happiness as a con- cept (specifying what it is and what it isn't), broken it down to discover what being happy means for you, sought to extend and expand it to all instances in your life, and identified the components of happiness in your life that you should acknowledge and build on. Realize that happiness knows no boundaries; it has to do with living a bigger life, larger than the one that is right in front of your nose.

Many happy people report that the kinder you are—the more you try to be a person who naturally does random acts of kindness—the happier you will become. Of course, you might not have the time, energy, resources, or desire to tackle big global issues. Nevertheless, there are many smaller situations close to home where you can do something for others and get outside yourself.

ASSIGNMENT

Start making acts of kindness something you do naturally. Being kind is hard to do when you aren't happy. If you force yourself to do a small nice act or two as an assignment, you will feel happier. Being kind to a fellow human being—from holding a door for a stranger to anonymously doing something for a friend or a colleague—shows God, the universe, Buddha, or whatever your conception of a higher power is that you are grateful. It's as if you said a little prayer of thanks for the things you have, but without words.

Q and A

Q. I've never been happy, so how do I do this chapter?

A. You are going to start looking for things that make you happy, or at least as close to it as possible. You'll be an experimenter, keeping an eye out for new feelings that may seem like odd combinations at first: feeling confident and sort of giddy, feeling optimistic and relaxed. Maybe you'll catch yourself swaggering or humming to yourself. Watch out for clichés about happiness; you'll be prone to latch on to them, and it's better to have your own personal definition. A couple of physical examples of holding the feeling is the dip in a dance and the fuzzy "high" feeling after getting a massage. Try to stay in that mind-set as long as you can, avoiding people who might burst the bubble.

Q. I don't want to feel fleeting happiness; I just want to feel good most of the time. Is this right?

A. Actually, there is a difference between happiness and contentment. When people say they want happiness, what they're really looking for is contentment, a feeling of satisfaction that does not go away when the outdoor concert, Sunday sermon, or nap is over. The peaceful, warm-all-over feeling of contentment comes with satisfaction and fulfillment that are not tied to specific events but rather are based on things that do not change, like close relationships, connecting to God (or your higher power), and feeling genuinely grateful.

Q. I understand that finding happiness within me is important, but can I also make myself happy from the outside? Can you give me examples of that? Is that cutting corners?

A. As long as you do both inside and outside work, it's fine. Making yourself happy from the outside is like going to a funny movie when you are in a bad mood. The simplest explanation for how this works is that laughing is a physical reaction that then simulates a mood. You can also accomplish this just by grinning or smiling.

Q. Can you give me a real-life example of starting to do "happiness math"?

A. You may think that you don't have enough happy seconds in your life that you can string together to make a happy moment, five minutes, or ten minutes. However, you might just not be aware of them. Think back: How many flickers of happiness did you have today, whether or not you acknowledged them? They might have been brief flashes, not earth-shaking bursts, but they were there.

Take an average morning in your life as an example. You woke up before your alarm went off by just a few minutes, which gave you a sense of contentment: you didn't have to hear the beeping, and you got up on your own, which was a small victory; it seems like the beginning of a good day. It's a small dollop of happiness, but it's there all the same. Then you shower and shave, nicking yourself once, and you become irritated when the schoolchildren on the street hold you up by blocking your path. You are annoyed by the time you arrive at the coffee shop, but your favorite barista is there and starts your coffee as soon as you come in the door. The special treatment feels nice—another droplet of happiness. It's so small, but it's there. The driver in front of you is slow, you miss a light, and you curse under your breath because you might be late. You park, walk into the lobby, then decide that you are going to take the stairs for exercise instead of waiting for the elevator, and at the third floor you give yourself a mental high-five for doing it. You walk into the office with a small grin on your face without realizing it.

Let's just start with that. Those were three small moments of happiness, no more than five to ten minutes. Now go from ten minutes a day to thirty minutes just by counting better or by developing more subtle antennae. Recognize and hold that feeling for as long as you can. You are on your way.

DAY TWELVE

Inertia and Momentum

Inertia is your biggest enemy. Your routine might not be comfortable, or it might be downright dull, but it is predictable, and people are wired to pick constancy over change—even when the change is for the better. When you try to switch things around or question the status quo, your body's reaction is to dig in its heels—even at a cellular level. Change of any kind takes a determined and concerted effort because you are, essentially, fighting yourself. My patients are often baffled and ask, "I know I have to do things differently; I know I have to get out of this situation and move on, but why is it so hard?"

Under pressure, some patients will take one step, make one attempt, and then stop at "good enough" when the crisis ends. As a result, they fall back into the relationship with the good-enough girlfriend or boyfriend or stay in the good-enough job with good-enough benefits, only to realize a few weeks later that they are really frustrated again. What happened? The answer is that they lost momentum.

Momentum is your best friend. Make sure that you notice when you are gliding, even if just for a few seconds; it's momentum that is carrying you along. You are out of the bad relationship, and you find yourself whistling. You've lost some weight, and for a moment you feel good-looking again. You read the want ads, and for a second you feel hopeful as you envision a new job. If you are on a roll, there's a little downhill momentum when you can take your feet off the pedals for a few seconds. Don't worry; recognizing momentum won't make it disappear. "Don't be greedy and want more," scoffs that censoring voice in your head. "Stop now, while you are ahead," it warns. However, I'll encourage you: don't slow down; keep plugging along.

Instances of momentum can be very subtle. Everyone has experienced the feeling of driving along, and suddenly it seems as if there are only green lights ahead; you are funnier than usual at a party, and the jokes and the punch lines flow effortlessly; the elevator doors open the second you hit the button to call it, and up you go.

By today, day 12, small accomplishments that you didn't notice before (because you didn't have the trained eye that you have now) will become evident. Perhaps you made the correct comment without pause, or you made the right choice without doubting yourself and you wanted to pat yourself on the back. You might have talked yourself down the other day, whereas before you'd have exploded; you got out of the kitchen quickly because you knew you'd overeat if you stayed; you felt a familiar sadness, recognized it, and then were able to let it go; you didn't beat yourself up when you normally would have done so. Whatever your small victory is, it has come about because of momentum. You are moving forward; the wheels are turning, and you are moving toward change. You are changing.

There are two psychological concepts at work here. The first is that success begets success; the second is that you yourself recognize your (small or large) triumphs and give yourself kudos for things going well. You can give yourself praise only if you feel responsible for the outcome.

In other words, take steps that you know will be successful, because they will motivate you to take more steps. When something does go right, pat yourself on the back, don't just brush it off and credit Lady Luck. Start moving, even if you do go around in a circle or two before you figure out which way is out. Stop waiting for change to come knocking on your door; start creating it yourself. We'll break all of this down into manageable instructions later.

Motivational speakers tell you to do what you really want to do *right now*, to stop putting it off. You protest (rightfully so), "Yeah, yeah, walk out on my job, tell my credit card bills to go to hell, and just jump on a jet plane to Bali. Just spin the globe and put my finger down on a spot. It's not going to happen." Who are these people who just walk out on life, throwing in the towel and doing what they *really* want to do instead, you wonder—and what exactly do they want to do instead?

The first problem, you declare, is that you are not very passionate about anything else—at least, not enough to leave your 401(k) and the vacation days you've patiently saved up. In the next sentence you'll try to talk both me and yourself out of making a change; it goes something like this: "It's going to get better. It's really not so bad. Most days I kind of like what I do. This is being a grown-up, and that isn't." Maybe you go back to the myth that a spark of motivation will flare up suddenly for you, just like people in infomercials who say, "I was just sick and tired of . . ." or "One day I woke up and just decided . . ."

Self-defeating thoughts will keep you inert and make you resistant to change. *You* have to start the momentum. Do something, anything, to start it; don't wait for it to come and sweep you off your feet. Run and slide. Once you have some motion, the hint of a breeze, take off on your glider or lean into the wind and use it to your advantage. All this means that you will take responsibility and not assume that when change is really meant to be, it will come from outside you, knocking at your door. The will to change has to come from within, and the practice of change has to come from without, until the two meet in the middle.

All of these explanations and instructions seem somewhat obvious, don't they? However, gone is that nice (but impossible) notion that you were just going to have a dramatic "Aha!" moment one day, when tears would stream down your face and you'd walk off into the sunset, a new and changed person. You now realize that you have to reprogram yourself, rewire your brain, and, in a nontraditional way, re-parent yourself.

Rewire and Re-parent

Many of your daily activities, good or bad, are habitual. The more you do them, the more deeply you etch the path into your brain. (Think of a path in the woods you take when hiking: each time you walk the same route, there is less resistance because there is less undergrowth to slow you down.) This means that as you start to rewire yourself—force yourself to do things differently—you have to create a new groove in your brain. It's pretty straightforward: do the desired activity over and over and over, knowing that you are working on a new neurological pathway.

Practicing silently, in your head, actually works, too. Every time you go through the motions in your head, the biochemical resistance along the thought path is reduced. In other words, the more times a mental event happens, the more likely it is to happen again, because you've rehearsed it, even if it was just in your mind's eye.

The concept of re-parenting is similar. Your parents trained you when you were a child, and now as an adult you must unravel what they did, if it isn't to your liking, and redo it yourself. You were young and impressionable under their care, and you had no choice but to follow. Whatever they inflicted on you, you've mourned it, you're in the process of healing it, or you are still upset about it.

As an adult you have a *choice* of doing it the way you were taught (or even brainwashed or coerced) or doing it a different way. Too many people, at this point in their lives, just shrug it off, having learned to be helpless, and don't exercise the choice to do things differently. Many decide to believe that the acquired ways of reacting are actually their own by now, so why bother. If the ways you learned to behave, react, and relate aren't working for you, you can carve out new ways of thinking and reacting. It's both strange and novel to think of emotional reactions or personality traits as ingrained habits, but they are.

Pulling yourself up and changing direction is difficult. Sometimes you can let the current move you along smoothly, reading and doing your assignments, knowing that a cumulative good result will eventually occur, but at other times you have to swim against the tide. Be tenacious about retooling a new reaction or habit, even if you haven't felt the glide of momentum in a while.

You can come back to this book and this chapter every time you get stuck. Every time you haven't had a glide in a while and are wondering if you are doomed to be mired wherever you are, revisit these pages. Whether this is the first or the tenth time you are reading this chapter, it will give you ideas to help you recognize, create, rewire, and re-parent yourself in order to become who you want to be.

To help you in this process, I am going to give you a list of rules and guidelines, then I'll expand on them in the pages to come:

1. Stop listing reasons you can't.

2. Name your goal.

3. Accept that understanding by elimination counts as therapeutic work.

4. Learn to recover.

5. Don't fear overshooting.

6. Stop believing that change will come to you from outside.

7. Don't let your psyche look for excuses not to do your writing work.

ASSIGNMENT

Now I'll go into detail about this list of rules. As you read the explanatory text, pause and check your reactions. Keep your pen and paper nearby and jot down whatever comes to mind, so you don't forget. Go back later and fill in the details and specifics.

1. Stop listing reasons you can't. You can't develop momentum because somewhere inside, you don't believe you can actually

do it (regardless of what you are telling me). Maybe you don't even want to afford yourself the luxury of visualizing your goal or your dream. Indulge me for a second here with a complete fantasy; just toy with the image that it could be. The sky won't fall down, you won't be punished by karma, and no one will double over laughing at you. When patients do this practice in therapy, they have told me that they know they fear creating a mental image because it will be bittersweet, or even painful, not to have it come true. Do it anyway. Here my patient usually sighs, "It's not that easy to put the 'why I can't' aside like that." Hear me out. This is going to be really tough. You will have to tolerate uncertainty, and I agree with you that it won't be easy. Nevertheless, you have to take this step at some point if you are going to have a chance at making things change.

2. Name your goal. This is going to sound as if it contradicts the previous item, but it's really just about using a different channel of your brain for problem solving. Stick with me here. Now, with brutal—and I do mean brutal—honesty, ask yourself if the goal is reasonable for you. Don't have a *yes* or *no* answer in mind. Which part of it is a big stretch, and which part of it, with some luck and hard work, is achievable? Is part of it within your grasp, but you just haven't reached out for it?

This is an exercise I do every day with every patient. What would your therapist be thinking when you are describing your goal? If I were sitting in front of you as you told me, I would carefully assess your goal in order to determine if it makes sense, given your personality, your strengths, and your weaknesses. Everyone needs to scrutinize whatever he or she is trying to accomplish and evaluate objectively whether, given the resources—time, place in life, support system—it's reasonable. This doesn't mean that you won't achieve a goal eventually, but is the one you are trying to tackle right now truly realistic? Or does it keep you in a constant state of yearning and, worst of all, immobile? Many people just sit and become comfortable pining away: they are comfortable being uncomfortable.

3. Accept that understanding by elimination counts as therapeutic work. In the decision-making process, if a choice you make isn't right, you eliminate it as an option and move on to the next possibility. It's a question of learning by doing: sometimes you do it right, and sometimes you do it wrong. Don't beat yourself up if you make the wrong choice; remember that elimination counts. Most people sulk because they can't redefine failure as part of the learning process. If you specify what you want, say it out loud, and keep bumping into things in the dark as you move along, you'll eventually find your way.

   Online dating has helped people that way: it makes them define what they want instead of just fantasizing that they'll run into the perfect person by chance. Your blunder isn't a failure; it's the elimination of what wasn't right. Just remember yourself as a child playing Marco Polo or Battleship. Every move brought you closer to your target, even if it wasn't the exact move you started with.

4. Learn to recover. When you're a grown-up and you're bruised or scratched, you might not have someone to tell you, "It's going to be all right," slap a bandage on it, and tell you to run along. Part of being grown up is that you have to whimper to yourself, find the first-aid kit by yourself, and feel pity all on your own. That feeling can throw you back to the third grade really fast. Sometimes there's a bump, or maybe you have a very different type of injury—an interaction that didn't go your way and that left you feeling slighted and angry, for example. Try saying "Oops." It's just one syllable, but it's such a great word: "Oops." Having a verbal equivalent of shrugging your shoulders or a visual one of letting something slide off you helps tremendously.

Suppose you are having a good day, and then you drop something—a folder, a box, a plastic container—and all of the contents go flying. You have a choice: you can become angry and curse at yourself, or you can just say "Oops" and keep moving. Save the anger and name-calling for a situation that really, really merits it. The overarching goal is to maintain a sense of internal balance, in which things that happen outside you don't jolt you emotionally. It's not about being an impenetrable rock; it's about being flexible and keeping perspective. It's a lifelong goal that takes a lot of practice, so be patient with yourself.

5. Don't fear overshooting. People most often aim too low, too hesitantly, and too short, for fear of overshooting. Something seems like less of a failure if you undershot: you didn't quite make it because you didn't give it your all; you weren't totally prepared. Think of doing a handstand or a headstand: you'd rather spend time trying to kick up than flail and fall over because you pushed too hard. However, when you overshoot, you actually get to the place you wanted to be, even if only for a nanosecond. Find examples in your life where you do this.

    Motivational speaker Les Brown puts it nicely: "Shoot for the moon, and if you miss it you will still be among the stars." Confucius said that if you shoot for the stars, you might hit the moon. The cautious seldom err; they don't hit the stars, the moon, or anything else. Rearrange the way you think so that you actually get to experience the handstand for just a second, even if you do fall down.

6. Stop believing that change will come to you from outside. Are you still waiting for the right diet to help you lose weight, the right man or woman to fix your commitment phobia, the right motivational speaker to

light a fire under you? Think hard about the part of you that is still holding back, hoping that someone else who just happens to be going in the same direction will take you along or that something else will "give" you inspiration. You might not know what to do about it this minute, but at least be honest with yourself. Maybe you don't need any of the things you think you do; or you just have to start going through the motions because waiting isn't getting you anywhere.

7. Don't let your psyche look for excuses not to do your writing work. "You are too busy to do this therapy junk," that little devil perched on your shoulder will whisper. "You are really fine just the way you are, so why are you rocking the boat? It is very self-centered of you to take all this time for yourself to yammer and write about yourself when you could be doing something constructive like fixing the caulking around the bathtub or taking out the garbage." Tell that little (or big) voice to back off and take a long hike off a short pier.

You've been on the receiving end of this; you know when you hear your friends make weak excuses. Don't be that person. Instead of whining and moping, figure out the practical work you have to do to get to where you want to be. No one thinks of being practical as something necessary for successful therapy. Therapy is supposed to be complex, emotional, and maybe even a bit magical—but practical? Practical is recipes under twenty minutes, figuring out TiVo so you can do two things at once, or arranging seating at a banquet so as few people as possible have contact with your annoying Uncle Jim or drunk Aunt Connie.

When you start hearing yourself making excuses, go back to thinking about practical solutions so that you can keep moving. Too often people in therapy neglect this, because it seems so obvious when dealing with a complex emotional issue. Do you feel yourself slowing down, doubting, or feeling sorry for yourself? Stop making excuses, do something practical from your therapeutic to-do list, and make sure, above all, that you keep writing until the dark cloud passes and you find more inspiration to take the next step.

Why Am I So Stuck?

The short answer to "Why am I so stuck?" is one that you might not actually hear in therapy, but it is the message that the therapist will try to get through to you in a more gentle way. Here's what the therapist is *actually* thinking:

Patient: I don't know if I actually caused these coincidences, these good things that are being offered to me. Maybe it's just luck. How do I know?

Therapist thinks: Who cares? Stop distracting yourself and move with the change. Take credit for it. What is the worst that can happen? Move on.

Patient: I can't decide. I've been sitting on this decision forever. I just can't decide which course to take.

Therapist thinks: Describe both right now; it helps you to decide, because you may hear that you describe one better than the other or realize that you feel better when you talk about one or the other. Pick one, pretend to commit emotionally, then tell me how you feel. Then pick the other and do the same. There will be a difference. Go.

Patient: Can I ever sit back in this process?

Therapist thinks: You can sit back and observe the buzz happening around you, as long as you stay alert and are taking inventory. Learn to watch your thoughts; watching your reactions is a sign that you are evolving psychologically. Just make sure that you know yourself well enough to recognize when you should stop sitting back and get back on the horse.

ASSIGNMENT

Your last assignment today is to recognize and maximize your momentum. If you can push and slide and push and slide until you get some traction, in time you'll own the change, and it will just follow you. Write about how you need to adjust your goals and refine your definition of yourself. As you think about visualizing your goals and the momentum you want to capture, pay close attention to your initial reaction. There are two things that will happen almost simultaneously, within milliseconds. First, you'll feel guarded and exasperated. Take note of that slight flash of a reaction; what is that about? Second, you'll feel hopeful and optimistic. That is the part of you that yearns for change. Tap into that. What is that about in this situation?

Q and A

Q. I wrote down that one of my goals is to have more freedom, but I can't put my finger on it in a practical way. Do you have any thoughts on this?

A. A definition of freedom that I particularly like is not having to rush or be irritated by the notion of not being on time. Think about it: if you never had to rush or be annoyed again, how liberating would that be? Keep your eye out for particular moments or situations when you feel free, light, or clear, and examine what the source is. Be inquisitive; experiment to figure out what it means to you personally.

Q. I have trouble giving myself praise, and I always thought that this was good because it has led me to have high standards. Is that true?

A. Pushing yourself is good, but many people don't pause long enough to recognize or enjoy their victories sufficiently. Ask yourself how much of your continuing to want more is just a knee-jerk reaction. It's impossible to live in and enjoy the present if you are always obsessed with a bigger, better deal in the future.

Q. I'm having a hard time bringing together the ideas of my mind and my brain and where my soul is, specifically. Any ideas?

A. One patient grappled with the idea that her soul was in her heart. We feel emotional pain in our gut, chest, or throat, and the discussion of where in your body your soul is housed is an ongoing one. There is a school of thought that believes that there are seven energy fields (called *chakras*) in the body that act as gateways to the soul. The mind-body debate is one of the central questions in the history of philosophy, so don't think that you are the only one who is pondering this. You shouldn't feel pressured to compartmentalize or delineate this in a concrete way immediately.

Q. How do I know if a new neurological pathway is being created?

A. A good example is if you find yourself on the way to the gym after work and you don't remember having pressured yourself to go, the way you have had to every day for the last two weeks.

Q. Is it true that happy people believe that good events are controllable and come from within themselves and that bad ones are both externally motivated and temporary?

A. Yes—all with some give and take, of course.

DAY THIRTEEN

The Fast Track

This chapter is about advanced concepts. It's like an upper-division college class for those of you who have made it through the basic requirements. You've survived; you're not a freshman anymore, and now you've signed up for the "experience required" lecture and assignments.

As you look at these concepts for the first time, consider your opinions. Some concepts may sound familiar, and you may think, "I already believe that" or "I already did that." Others will be brand-new to you. In either case, it is time to step up the pace.

These concepts are advanced because in therapy you usually don't start to think about them until you are well into the process. Only after you have been able to vent, organize, prioritize, and visualize your goals do you have the ability to delve into these complex, spiritual, and multidimensional topics. Here, then, is the complete list of advanced concepts that you have to keep in mind now and later.

1. Your brain, the two- to three-pound convoluted wrinkled mass that sits behind your face, is an organ that has to be maintained like a well-oiled machine in order to function properly. The idea that your brain just turns on and off on its own, puttering along just fine without any attention being paid to it, is very backward. Think of the many ways in which you take care of your body: you have an annual physical; your teeth are cleaned, straightened with braces, and whitened; you have your eyes tested for glasses and screened for glaucoma; you eat extra fiber to keep your colon healthy and have an annual colonoscopy.

   What do you do for your brain? Every year your family doctor asks you the routine checkup questions, which might include one general inquiry about your head or your brain. You answer that everything up there is about the same, apart from a passing hangover or headache. Over the past few years, however, you've been hearing more about brain health. Discussions of autism and learning disabilities are no longer for the specialists. Articles abound on your brain on drugs, memory problems and your brain, why your brain needs more oxygen, and exercising your brain. Best sellers explore the subject (two of my favorites are *The Female Brain* by Louise Brizendine, and *Change Your Brain, Change Your Life* by Daniel Amen).

   Therapy is for your mind, but you also have to make sure that the organ that houses it is in good shape. Start thinking of your brain as another body part that you have to take care of on a regular basis. Drink more water, watch more intelligent television programs, and get enough sleep. Do it as part of your overall health program, whether it's sending more oxygen up there by speeding up your heart rate, timing yourself on crossword puzzles, nurturing your creative self, or wearing headgear when required.

2. Be present. Be alert. *Be in the now.* That sounds great, you say, but what does "Be in the now" really mean? It means you should stop zoning out. It means that instead of thinking about the past or planning for the future, you focus on the present, whatever you are doing *right now.* It sounds easy, but once you check yourself, you'll find that you are either internally grumbling and rehashing the past or constantly running through a list of what you have to do tomorrow, next week, and next year.

   Being in the now unquestionably takes mental discipline, and the psychological benefits are huge: you remember more because you are paying attention to your present-day actions and surroundings, you savor the good experiences to their fullest, you end up with an improved ability to concentrate (it's like resistance training for the mind). Being able to stay in the present will enable you to know and monitor exactly what is going on inside you. The result is a physically and psychologically healthier you. People find it perfectly natural to repair physical damage immediately, but when it comes to the metaphysical, their inner world, they don't know what to do. To start practicing this, pause and check in with your body and mind.

In meditation classes you are taught to focus on your breathing. It sounds easy, but try it. How many breaths can you take before your mind wanders? You aren't as much in control of your mind as you thought, are you? The practice of focusing on your breathing and checking in with yourself often throughout the day will enable you to start being more in the present. The payoff is being able to intervene before you get stressed out, sick, or injured, as well as having better control of your emotions.

3. Accept that you are a product of where you came from and that you have the ability to make the choice not to be that way anymore. Understand on a very deep level that you might have been a child without choices, that you had the decisions and plans of others inflicted upon you, but that the present is very distinct and you don't have to be a victim of your past. You are an adult and can choose to react any way you want.

   The alteration that a tethered baby elephant undergoes to become an older elephant that decides it wants to sit in the shade and so just moves under the tree is an easy concept to grasp, but it is hard for a human to fully execute a similar change. Understand that you don't have to do this in an angry, reactive way ("When my dad drank, we all had to tiptoe around the house, so I'm never walking on eggshells again!").

   Rather, you can incorporate it in a more intellectual way, such as by coming to the conclusion that you have been shopping for more and more stuff to fill an archaic void, so you are going to decide not to continue this habit. Perhaps you become aware that you choose high-maintenance partners because your parents demanded so much care and attention, so now you decide to break the chain. You might finally realize that it's not a twist of fate that you keep running into one bossy supervisor after another; rather, you have a problem with authority figures that goes back to your overbearing, controlling mother.

After you've done the work in the earlier chapters—venting about this topic, putting its details in chronological order, and healing in whatever way you choose—you can decide to do things differently. You have that option—take it.

4. Make time for yourself. You not only deserve it, it is critical for your well-being. Many people use the excuse that they don't have room in their schedules to go to therapy or to make a commitment to activities that are good for the brain, the mind, and the soul. "I have too many people counting on me," they say. If you can't cook the family dinner, attend an event from start to finish, or do the laundry, what will happen? Nothing will happen, or perhaps somebody else will do it.

Others have the opposite reaction: What good will forty-five minutes a day of reading and working through this book, seeing a therapist, or just meditating and breathing do for you and those around you? The answer is an exponential amount of good. Until you come to the conclusion that your family or your job can spare you for an hour a day without combusting and that you deserve a small chunk of time for yourself, you won't be able to move toward change. The commitment is crucial to your growth and your sanity.

5. There is no such thing as closure. People throw the word *closure* around as if it's something you buy at a hardware store. You are finished with a relationship, are at peace with a death, or have accepted the presence of a difficult person in your life. Somehow we think that that moment actually comes with the click of a closing door. It might be the moment we sigh, suddenly realizing that she's not going to change, I'm never going to see him again, we aren't meant to be together. Frequently, however, you find yourself getting angry, protesting, "I'm not getting closure," and huffing to your therapist, "I still don't have closure."

In therapy, we discuss the fact that you want clarity, hard definitions, right and wrong, black and white, good guy–bad guy—no gray fuzzy areas, please. However, the whole obsession with closure is a control issue. "It's over," you say, trying to convince yourself that your strained relationship with a parent, your grieving for a deceased friend, or your pining over an ex is finished. You want to feel in control of your life again. Unfortunately, the emotional brain doesn't work that way; the memories linger and anniversary dates bring them up again.

Learning to live with ambiguity is a choice, and one day you might actually achieve what you've been calling closure, but not if you keep checking, like peeking under a bandage to see if a wound has healed. The relationship, the memories, and the event won't change or disappear, but you'll finally become tired of letting them beat you up, or of beating up on them, and you'll decide on acceptance. Then you'll call it closure. Don't think about it as a destination you are waiting to get to or an exit that you are keeping an eye out for while driving. There is no closure, only process.

6. Being humble is sexy. You never see that on the cover of a magazine, but it's true. When people are in the patient's seat across from me, they often describe humility as an attractive characteristic. You develop humility by being grateful. How can you honestly be thankful, you might ask, without feeling as if it is something you have to check off a list?

The easiest way to get to this point is to do volunteer work. It can be formal volunteer work through an organization, just being nice and checking in with an elderly neighbor, donating money to "virtually" adopt an animal, or helping someone in another part of the world start a small business by lending him or her the same amount of money you'd spend on going to the movies and buying a tub of popcorn. Signing up for a two-year commitment to be a big brother or big sister is great, but don't keep putting off doing something generous because it's overwhelming.

Make volunteering or donating, and not just the act of putting change in a Salvation Army bucket at Christmas, part of your life. The feelings and emotions that giving confers are impossible to achieve in any other way: you truly gain perspective on how lucky you are, you are sincerely thankful and not just giving lip service, and you see yourself as part of the bigger picture and not just the star of your own epic film about you, you, you. Volunteering or giving back is a requirement that I make for therapy. It also helps you to become a more complete and interesting person. Until you do it, you won't know; I can't explain to you what the experience will be like. Just take my word for it.

7. Don't underestimate the importance or the rewards of being practical. No one thinks of practicality as a quality that you need in order to be successful in therapy. Practical is pedestrian. Therapy is supposed to be complex, emotional, maybe a bit magical—but practical? What are the concrete steps you need to take to get from here to there? People in therapy frequently neglect this part, because it seems so obvious when dealing with a complex emotional issue. You can't go to the gym because you didn't bring shorts to work? Get a locker, then you won't have that excuse again. Are you having a strained relationship with a coworker who does too much loud talking on the telephone? Wear earplugs or an iPod for part of the day. Are you sick of having lunch with your stepmother? Go to a movie with her instead. These are all issues that people have brought to therapy to talk about, and even though the deeper reasons have to be discussed, the immediate discomfort can be lessened by some practical problem solving.

8. The somewhat flippant-sounding idea of forgiving being a staple of the healing process has left many people confused. It isn't so simple, they moan. The act of forgiving may be approached with a high and mighty "I'm so enlightened spiritually that I can do this" attitude, which has more to do with coping than really forgiving and letting go. If you had an abusive brother, an absent father, or an alcoholic mother who isn't asking for forgiveness, it's really, really hard to do it in a one-sided way. Just know that forgiving is a lot harder than it's been made out to be. You try to forgive and you want to feel relieved,

but you might find that you feel skeptical, annoyed, perplexed, or just sad. Forgiving or making amends is not an act; it's a process.

9. Define your own successful relationships. Although we talked about relationships and interactions with parents earlier, this concept of successful relationships merits a second visit in our discussion of advanced topics. Our society is ripe with very staunch shoulds and shouldn'ts, but it's obvious to any experienced couples therapist that Dr. and Mrs. Huxtable or Mr. and Mrs. Brady do not exist; and if they do, they might be separated, divorced, have an open marriage, or spend most of the time ignoring each other. (It is interesting to note that in the original script the character Carol Martin, who married Mike Brady, was divorced, but the network thought that the public could not deal with that.)

Having your significant other be your soul mate, your best friend, your partner, and your parent all rolled into one, with an unvarying amount of lifelong lust to boot, is a myth. The quick changes and adjustments in relationships that you see on TV are almost impossible. Most of the problems people grapple with are related to their parents, and the parents' problems, in turn, came from their parents. The situation requires more than one hourlong session to be resolved.

Think about how relating to your lover or partner is influenced by your relationship with your parents. How you get along with authority figures, from your micromanaging boss to the police officer who pulls you over for speeding, is directly related to how you got along with the first grown-ups in your life.

Your relationship with the parent of the opposite sex influences how you view people of the opposite sex. Untangling that conundrum of transference reactions while simultaneously attempting to formulate a definition that works for you about your lovers, partners, or spouse is super-challenging.

10. Be Zen. There are numerous ways of thinking that come under this one term. Let's look at just a few:

- Don't consider any experience a waste of time: there is a lesson in every one. Your last relationship wasn't for naught; it taught you many things that you would never have learned had you not lived through it. Six months with the supervisor from hell was a tutorial on how to deal with difficult people. Now you know firsthand what works and what doesn't with obstructive types. It's hard to think that every experience is positive, that every cloud has a silver lining, but after you're done feeling sorry for yourself, switch channels and try it. You survived and you grew; therefore you can handle it.

- Do not be attached to an outcome. This is a very complex notion; exactly what does it mean? In short, invest 100 percent effort in everything you do, but if something doesn't turn out exactly the way you envisioned it, accept that the result was in some way meant to happen, and your scenario just wasn't in the cards. How many times have you thought back on an experience and said, "Yeah, I was upset then, but now, looking back, it's good that it went the way it did"?

- No experience or situation is inherently bad or good. You are the one who decides what adjective you are going to use to describe it. You can make an intellectual decision about how you are going to react to a situation. It's the same kind of decision you make when you're deciding whether you want french fries or mashed potatoes. Making a decision with your head and not being pushed into being irrational or dramatic by your emotions is a hard concept to understand and harder yet to put into practice, but the effect is invaluable.

ASSIGNMENT

Where are you in relation to these advanced concepts? Be honest. Which ones do you understand, even though you know you're not really a stellar candidate for them? Make this assignment a long-term wish list. Make a list of these ten concepts and determine what stage you are at with each one, then elaborate on what you need to do to make it yours.

Therapy, at this advanced point, is a question of routinely going through these concepts and nudging yourself forward, using the strategies you have learned and the tools you have acquired. Assess how far you've come, take note of where you've gotten stuck, do the emotional problem solving we've been doing together, and try it again, in a different way, never beating yourself up because you're not moving fast enough. After tomorrow, you'll be doing things at your own pace.

You have the tools and you know the type of exercise that works for you: free-associating until you come upon the answer, asking friends for feedback, delineating the concrete steps that take you from where you are to where you want to be, or just making lists that help you to prioritize. Put these advanced concepts into that format, then put yourself into the picture. Concretize, and remember that you learned that *specificity* is the name of the game: What was the specific situation that made you realize you were too quick to brand something as a bad experience? When did you feel like a victim without pausing to remind yourself you are a grown-up with choices? When did you expect yourself to be alert despite the fact that you hadn't had the amount of sleep your brain requires?

ASSIGNMENT

Now we'll do some work on relationships and forgiveness. Ask yourself what you bring out in people. Of whom do they remind you? Of whom do you remind them? Have you ever had a relationship that makes no sense in reality? Maybe you remind your boss of his insolent son, and he reminds you of your controlling father, and even though nothing wrong has transpired at work, you are like oil and water together. You either repeat the same behavior or you work as hard as you can to go in the very opposite direction.

Write about siblings and birth order, friendships and love, communication, the parent to whom you were the most similar. How you think about gender and about men and women begins to develop at a very early age. What are your expectations of your significant other? Your concept of relationships comes from seeing your parents struggle with theirs. Do you shake your head and say, "I will never do it like they did," or do you wonder how they did some things so well, given what they were struggling with in their lives?

In the context of all these relationships, think about forgiveness, consider the following, and write about each:

1. Acknowledge your fantasy of the other people involved being part of the decision. Would they agree that they've been petty and heartless? Would they cry and hug you?

2. Examine the act of forgiveness. Rather than forgive others in a holier-than-thou way, especially when it doesn't come from a heartfelt conviction, aim more toward accepting them, being tolerant and understanding. Then take it a step further, being more realistic by saying to yourself, "What happened isn't going to change. Their attitudes will probably never change, I'm going to deal with it in an adult way because I choose to do so." Then set good boundaries and protect yourself from whatever toxicity they ooze.

3. Consider acts of random kindness. Have you ever become annoyed with someone in line who is not moving forward? You point it out, gritting your teeth at the stupidity, and then

the person smiles and says, "Oh, thanks." Your anger melts when you see that this is a real person, just like you, who happens to have become distracted. It's a good practice to assume that most people who do seemingly obnoxious things are either distracted or absorbed by their own worries; they are not trying to be stupid or ruin your day. The balm of human kindness will always smooth out the unnecessary wrinkles of a difficult moment, and it will leave you feeling a lot better—in fact, rather magnanimous.

4. Refuse to be a martyr; soften on the inside rather than tensing up. When you have a stubborn grandparent who won't stop complaining or a neighbor who won't let go of a grudge, just say to yourself, as you'd like to say to them, "I know deep down inside you probably have a good heart, so I'm going to try to let all this garbage about you go, because it's coming from somewhere else that has nothing to do with me."

A few parting words of wisdom: Zen is not something you can *decide* to be. It's something you have to *do*, like stretching every day. Some days you are psychically flexible and are able to reach a little farther; other days you feel stiffer and more distant than ever from putting your hands on the floor. Eventually the tips of your fingers will graze the floor. A nice stretch always feels so good.

Q and A

Q. What is the saying that you personally use to inspire yourself when things go wrong?

A. "In chaos there is opportunity"; that is, out of every chaotic situation can spring an unexpected and surprisingly favorable outcome.

Q. I keep hearing the word *Zen* used in a popular way. Can you tell me about it?

A. Zen, a school of thought of Mahayana Buddhism, was first documented in China in the seventh century and established a presence in North America and Europe in the late nineteenth and early twentieth centuries. Zen favors direct, experiential realization. The term is the Japanese translation of the Chinese word *Chan* and has found its way into the common vernacular, often used in place of *laid-back* or *cool*.

Q. You mentioned transference. What is that, exactly?

A. You project your feelings about someone from your past (such as a parent) onto another person in the present (such as your therapist), all the time unaware that your reaction is more about you than about this other person. Your emotional past is calling the shots in your present world. When you see a pattern emerge in how you deal with supervisors or younger colleagues, ask yourself if they remind you of someone. It's possible that the former is related to your relationship with your parents and the latter to your relationship with your younger siblings.

Q. I don't have time to do volunteer work—any suggestions?

A. There are many organizations, all easily found online, to which you can contribute without getting out of your chair, where you can help disadvantaged children, disabled adults, or even foster a dog or a cat.

Q. You mention repeating "the same behavior or [working] as hard as you can to go in the very opposite direction." Can you give me an example?

A. You become a lawyer to please your dad, who is a lawyer or always wanted to be one, or you do the opposite: you become a hippie artist because your parents are both military personnel. This is an extremely simple example; break it down into subtle dynamics when you look at your own life.

DAY FOURTEEN

Happily Ever After?

Finishing therapy is one of the most bizarre graduation events there is. You are partly proud, partly relieved, and partly perplexed that you've been kicked out of the therapeutic nest. In the ideal situation, you and your therapist decide together that you're finished, that you're ready to graduate. Sometimes your main issue has been resolved; at other times it has led to further concerns, and you've dealt with them as well—or will continue to do so at your own pace. Maybe you'll make an appointment from time to time for "tune-ups." Therapists occasionally even do phone sessions for patients who need to touch base and who have moved or travel for work.

In a few pages you'll be finished. You'll do your stream-of-consciousness writing for today, fill in the sentences, answer the questions, and experience a mixture of relief and pride at what both a meandering and a jolting ride this has been. This course was set up for you to learn how to examine and unravel your psychological questions yourself; it's a blueprint or a road map for traversing the minefields of your emotional problems and issues. Maybe now you'll consider taking them to a therapist, a support group, or a dance-therapy class.

Perhaps you'll read this book a second time and study the exercises that at one point seemed so difficult, and do the ones that you skipped the first time around (you think I didn't notice?). I hope that you'll bear in mind the books I recommended, do some kind of volunteer work to get better perspective, put "take care of brain" on your list of things to do, and call yourself on slacking when it is appropriate. Achieving your new goals will lead you to be a more self-aware person. At this point, writing every day, or almost every day, should give you a sense of being proactive about your mental health.

This is the last chapter, so get to work! It's the day for final exams and assignments in this course, so grab your pencil and paper, take a deep breath, and get moving.

ASSIGNMENT

As you think about the past two weeks, pick the answers (there can be more than one) that describe your experience with this book:

1. When I picked up this book I was hoping to

   a. Get an idea of what sort of things happen in therapy—behind closed doors—and what people actually talk about when they see their psychologists or counselors.

b. Start addressing certain problems that are really private, that I wanted to start to figure out but wished to do on my own, without anyone helping me at first.

c. Get a handle on some issues that have been ongoing for me. I wanted to make sure that I had really hashed out everything and left no stone unturned.

d. Do something for my mind, for my emotional well-being, without making an appointment with a therapist (because of money issues, lack of insurance coverage, or time constraints).

2. One thing that happened that I didn't expect was that

a. I could actually free-associate and write in a stream-of-consciousness sort of way, and sometimes go on for several pages.

b. At times I became very emotional, and my reactions surprised me. I was shocked that the simple act of writing could cause me to experience such profound feelings.

c. The tangle of things within me began to unravel and finally became more comprehensible.

d. I realized that psychological change wasn't some magical thing that was going to happen *to* me and that in fact there was a lot I could do to bring about change.

e. The big issue that has been weighing me down my whole life and coloring my world seemed a little less daunting and more manageable.

f. The writing made me feel relieved, as if I could check off having done something that was good for me.

g. In hindsight I became aware of issues that I had been either denying or minimizing.

3. An important piece of information that I gathered from the exercise of asking those around me for feedback was that

a. My friends and family are too nice. They didn't give me the sort of feedback that would really be helpful. Maybe they thought I was too sensitive or fragile, but now I have to seek out more hard feedback about how I present myself to the world.

b. I was unaware of the behaviors that were giving people the wrong impression of me. I obviously have to work harder to synchronize who I am inside with how I present myself.

c. It was embarrassing! If I hadn't asked, I really wouldn't have known how people perceive me. It was hard to hear, but it was good information. It was difficult not to brush it off or get angry, but I realize that it's incredibly useful knowledge, even if it wasn't pretty.

4. In writing my history, I had forgotten or minimized the importance of so many events. For example:

a. How truly messed up my family was. I thought they were within a normal range. When I started describing and listing certain behaviors and characteristics, I realized that I am lucky to have come out as okay as I did.

    b. How profoundly birth order affected how I define myself.

    c. That it was not my family, but the other people around me—friends or coworkers—who made impressions on me growing up.

    d. How addicted, volatile, or self-involved my mom or dad was.

    e. How absent or emotionally unresponsive my mom or dad was.

5. I'm sure that my power statement will change as I continue to develop and grow. It focuses me, it calms me, and it also

    a. Reminds me that I can't just take feeling balanced for granted.

    b. Helps me when I am spinning out of control.

    c. Reminds me that I can get answers by looking inward rather than outward. I have learned that I have to take a breath and close my eyes rather than panic and search outside myself for answers.

    d. Helps me to hold on to the good habits I am trying to develop rather than revert to the bad ones that are so easy to fall back on.

6. I continue to mourn and yet be puzzled by several incidents in my life that are

    a. Still fuzzy. I accept that I have to write about them as much as I can in order to understand my interpretation of them. More than anything, I must make sure that they aren't unconsciously hurting me in the present.

   b. Complicated. I wish they were black white because they'd be easier to understand. There are lots of shades of gray, feelings of ambivalence with which I have to learn to deal.

   c. Painful, and it's tough to revisit them. I'd rather not, but I know that I have to do so because they are coming out in unhealthy ways.

   d. Issues that I took for granted, believing that everyone has to deal with them. I just bottled them up and kept moving. It has ended up hurting me, in the long run.

7. Having been pleasantly surprised by how sensible a plan can be for dealing with emotional problems or for personal growth, my favorite recommendation is to

   a. Make a detailed list of steps that have to be taken.

   b. Do something creative or even silly to get over the bump that is in the way.

   c. Make a decision to change the way I think. Just a simple act, like saying, "I am not going to see it that way anymore," makes a difference.

   d. Make the advanced concepts mine. I understand most of them, but when I look at my life I see that they are not integrated. Integration is a challenge.

8. One thing that still lingers, and that I am going to have to dig deeper to reach, is

   a. Being honest with myself in my writing. Calling myself on lying or exaggerating. Calling myself on substituting bravado for real strength.

b. Knowing that new patterns of acting or think-ing take effort, that they don't come naturally, that I have to do the new action or think the new thought repeatedly so that it creates a new neurological pathway in my brain.

c. Not being fearful of change. Asking myself what is the worst that can happen, then making plans to ensure that it won't happen rather than just living in fear that it might.

ASSIGNMENT

Answer the following questions:

1. On which of the fourteen days did you catch yourself slacking off?

2. For which specific topic did you do the bare minimum, then turn the page as quickly as possible? Maybe you figuratively threw up your hands and said to yourself, "I understand this pretty well, and that is good enough for me right now."

3. At which point did you take a deep breath, sigh, and think, "I am not ready to tackle this one right now"?

4. When did you find yourself absolutely baf-fled, as if I were speaking to you in a foreign language and no matter how many times you read it, it made no sense?

5. Sit in the therapist's seat for a moment and ask what topic did your patient (you) gloss over or seem a little shallow in responding to, and why do you think this happened?

ASSIGNMENT

This is a two-part assignment. First, ask yourself the following: What do you want to accomplish in the next six months? What do you want to accomplish next year? In the next ten years? Do you need a boost in writing about this? Pretend that it's your birthday or New Year's Eve or that something has happened to make you realize that life is too short.

Second, sit in the therapist's seat for a moment and look back. Consider the person who started reading on day 1 and look at the work completed up until day 14. What does this person need to work on to become the person that he or she wants to be?

Q and A

Q. I don't want to go to therapy, because I don't want to become dependent on my therapist. Could I end up in therapy forever and not be able to make a decision on my own?

A. A good therapist-patient relationship encourages clear communication and mutual respect. It doesn't promote dependence, although while you are learning in the beginning, it might feel that way a little. A good therapist, like this book, will teach you a process, not make you "addicted" to or dependent on him or her forever. You also should give the therapist feedback on what works for you and what you expect.

Q. What can I add to my daily stream-of-consciousness writing in order to move things along?

A. Any movie or book that sparks a thought or a topic for you. One of my favorite movies is *Murderball*, a documentary about paraplegic athletes. It's impossible to watch without having strong feelings. It's an incredible catalyst for this process.

Your Checklist

In one way or another, in the past two weeks you have learned about psychology, human behavior, neurology, change and motivation theory, family dynamics, and more. Now I want you to actually check off some of the steps you have taken. Remember that I told you to recognize your accomplishments and not only focus on things left to do? That's what this exercise is about.

In reading the following list, don't brush any item off as trivial. Pat yourself on the back for the ones you recognize and acknowledge as your accomplishments. Maybe the learning has been dramatic, or perhaps a very small seed has been planted. You may even feel better because you knew there was a void in your life, or you had a feeling of dread, wrongdoing, or ill-defined fears that kept you from being content with your life, and now you don't feel so alone in your conviction. You have a plan for how to deal with it, or at least for starting the process.

Put a checkmark next to each item that resonates with you. In the preceding chapters you might have written in the margins as you read and reflected. If you didn't the first time around, next time do write down words or thoughts that are even remotely relevant. For now, put checks, circles, and stars on the pages as you think about your progress.

- Venting and free-associating help me chronicle my day; they help me to unwind, organize my thoughts, and purge. Just as I would vent in therapy, I let myself jump from thought to thought in my writing without doing a spell-check or worrying about punctuation. It allows my brain to relax.

- Putting my story into words, scene by scene, as I delve into my past, gives me a sense of my life that I never had before. Memories have popped up that I haven't recalled in years. How I got to where I am now makes more sense. Events look somewhat linear; where I am now makes more sense to me.

- I understand that my acknowledging is similar to a therapist's reflecting. I am starting to recognize subtle reactions and feelings more easily, taking note and accepting what the feeling *is* rather than ignoring it or brushing it off as unimportant.

- Giving myself permission to take time to write—to think or just take a couple of deep breaths—makes me feel steady and more balanced. Checking in with myself comes under the theme of taking care of my brain like any other part of my body.

- I've started to understand the basic psychological concepts that people deal with in face-to-face therapy. There are lots of them. They are worth weeks, months, and even years of therapy. I'll continue doing my own work at my own pace, whether it's picking up recommended reading or doing my daily journal entries.

- Asking people around me for feedback was challenging; I might never do it so formally again. Now I have better antennae; I listen for feedback more closely in conversation. It is important to know how I portray myself. I am training myself to listen for verbal and nonverbal cues. Information on how I come off to others is around me constantly; I just have to let my defenses down in order to be able to hear it.

- I can resist the temptation to define myself by my habits, my place in my family's birth order, or who I was told I was as a child. I have free will; I react not to please or annoy others but to communicate and connect, to share and consequently to grow in relationships in a mature and adult fashion.

- I now am able to recognize and take advantage of psychological momentum rather than stopping and sitting down once I've accomplished something. I know how to keep moving, hoping to get better traction.

- I've become creative in thinking of metaphors for change. I can identify problems that still get in my way, I have a sense of how to think outside the box and create the kind of ritual that will allow me to resolve issues and get them out of my system.

- I have specified my personal goals. I have work goals, relationship goals, career goals, and family goals. Never before did I write down my goals so specifically for my brain, my mind, my soul, and my body. I've come up with steps to take to reach my goals—practical ones. I know that I am a work in progress and that I have to be inventive to reach my aspirations.

- I know that I have to create neurological pathways in order to reinforce new patterns of behavior. Understanding the difficult mechanism of creating a new habit, and being aware of how easy it is to fall back on old ones, makes me more tenacious.

- I've broken down any change that I want to effect into manageable steps. I initially thought this would be simple, but it wasn't. Now I know I have to put a determined effort into quantifying my objectives into manageable actions that are realistic so that I don't become overwhelmed or distracted.

- I have a power statement. Sometimes it sounds like the ones that pro athletes use when they are psyching themselves up. Parts of it sound New Agey, and other parts are very prayerlike. It complements my personality, however, and I recite it out loud at least once a day because it calms and focuses me.

- I've tackled the biggest issue: I know that being able to label myself and my patterns of behavior is only part of the process. Now I must keep the momentum going; I have learned that understanding isn't an excuse for stopping, it's precisely the moment at which I have to buckle down and start planning change.

- I know how to call myself on self-sabotage. I recognize when I'm being lazy, scared, or satisfied with "good enough." I might be like that again sometimes, but I know that eventually I have to get back to my program.

- I've studied the advanced concepts. Now I'm letting them sink in a little, then I'm going to reread them, determining which ones resonate with me already and which are going to take some long-term effort.

You have been your own therapist for the past two weeks. Maybe you leaped at the chance to get into your own psyche, or maybe you just dusted off some tough memories and took a trepidant step forward. Still, it was a step forward. It was movement in the right direction that didn't require an appointment, permission from your insurance company, or hand holding from someone who is worried about, or angry with, you.

Though tomorrow you won't have a specific assignment in this book, you can almost spontaneously at this point give yourself one. Ask yourself: What am I worried about today? What did I do well that I will give myself well-deserved credit for? What pattern am I still falling into even though my logical brain knows it makes no sense? You know now that growing psychologically is a process, one you have to keep challenging yourself to work at. You can continue to do it yourself tomorrow, and the day after.

EPILOGUE

Keeping Your Grip

Get a Grip is a composite of the experiences of hundreds of patients, intertwined with psychological, medical, and spiritual theories. My inspiration in writing has been to demonstrate to you, the reader, how resilient, creative, and unapologetically stubborn the human psyche can be.

Can individuals ask themselves probing psychological questions, then answer them in a way that heals and inspires change? I think so, and I am confident that you have to ability to do so. Trust your instincts, be firm in your belief that the topics you have found yourself writing about consistently or furiously since day 1 are important enough to merit your undivided attention. After two weeks of this program, your clinical intuition is sharper than it's ever been. From this point on, you get to choose the questions you ask yourself.

Right now shouldn't be the only time you reach this part of the book. Use the process you've learned in order to problem-solve every time you have a concern that involves your heart, your soul, your spirit, your emotions, your mind, your brain, your relationships, and your goals in life. Expect great changes, even if you need to work through this book twice or three times. Make this book your story, and aim to make your therapeutic goals grand and life changing.

You have the answers inside you. You just have to ask yourself the right questions.

REFERENCES

Amen, Daniel. *Change Your Brain, Change Your Life: The Breakthrough Program for Conquering Anxiety, Depression, Obsessiveness, Anger, and Impulsiveness.* New York: Three Rivers Press, 1999.

Brizandine, Louise. *The Female Brain.* New York: Random House, 2006.

Cameron, Julia. *The Artist's Way: A Spiritual Path to Higher Creativity.* Los Angeles: Jeremy P. Tarcher/Perigee, 1992.

Ensler, Eve. *The Vagina Monologues.* New York: Random House, 2001.

Ferriss, Tim. *The Four-Hour Work Week: Escape 9–5, Live Anywhere, and Join the New Rich.* New York: Random House, 2007.

Finney, Jack. *The Body Snatchers.* Laurel, NY: Lightyear Press, 1993.

García Márquez, Gabriel. *One Hundred Years of Solitude.* New York: HarperCollins, 2006.

Gilbert, Elizabeth. *Eat Pray Love: One Woman's Search for Everything across Italy, India and Indonesia.* New York: Penguin, 2007.

Headley, Maria. *The Year of Yes*. New York: Hyperion, 2006.

Lee, Harper. *To Kill a Mockingbird*. New York: HarperCollins, 2002.

Sacks, Oliver. *Musicophilia: Tales of Music and the Brain*. New York: Knopf, 2007.

Tolstoy, Leo. *War and Peace*. New York: Knopf, 2007.

INDEX

221